PERFECT PAGES
Self Publishing with Microsoft Word
— Aaron Shepard —

Nowadays, new technologies and services have made it easier than ever to publish your book. But if you mean to design it yourself, you may face an important question: Do I need an expensive page layout program like Adobe InDesign, Adobe PageMaker, or QuarkXPress? Or can I instead use a word processor like Microsoft Word?

If you know the basic principles of typography and book design—as well as the abilities of your program—there's no reason a book done in Word should look less than professional. With this book as guide, you'll soon produce pages no reviewer will scoff at.

"On target . . . . Concisely addresses a lot of topics that Word users need to know about."

James Felici, author,
The Complete Manual of Typography

"Excellent not only as a guide to using Word to design books, but also as a concise guide to book design."

Morris Rosenthal, author,
Print-on-Demand Book Publishing

Also by Aaron Shepard

Aiming at Amazon
The NEW Business of Self Publishing

The Business of Writing for Children
An Award-Winning Author's Tips on
Writing Children's Books and Publishing Them

PERFECT PAGES

Self Publishing with Microsoft Word

OR

How to Avoid High-Priced Page Layout Programs or
Book Design Fees and Produce Fine Books in
MS Word for Desktop Publishing and
Print on Demand

Aaron Shepard

Shepard Publications
Olympia, Washington

Author portrait by Wendy Edelson

ISBN-13: 978-0-938497-33-2
ISBN-10: 0-938497-33-2

Library of Congress Control Number: 2005908259
Library of Congress subject headings:
Desktop publishing
Self-publishing—Handbooks, manuals, etc.
Publishers and publishing—Handbooks, manuals, etc.
Microsoft Word
Book design
Type and type-founding
Word processing

1.11

For Further Help

Though Aaron is glad to receive feedback from readers, he cannot provide private technical assistance with Word. For further help, please see the resources listed at the end of this book or on his Web site.

Made in Microsoft Word!

The pages and cover of this book were created in Microsoft Word 2004 and converted to PDF with Adobe Acrobat 7. Graphics were prepared in Adobe Photoshop Elements 2. Production was done on a Mac in OS X.

The text font is 12-point Georgia, set with 15-point line-spacing. The cover font is Verdana, with hand kerning.

All copies of the book are produced as print on demand by Lightning Source, Inc.

Contents

About This Book   9

Working with Word #1:
   Choosing a Version   **12**

1   Managing Word   13

    Managing Updates   14
    Managing Options or Preferences   15
    Managing the Workspace   18
    Managing Automatic Changes   20
    Managing Features   21
    Managing Old Files   22
    Managing Safety   23
    Managing Memory   25

Working with Word #2:
   Using Views   **26**

2   Formatting Your Document   29

    Setting Up Your File   30
    Setting Your Page Size   31
    Setting Your Page Margins   33
    Setting Up Sections   35
    Setting Up Headers and Footers   39
    Setting Up Columns   40

**Working with Word #3:
Using Templates**   **41**

3   Typesetting Your Text   43

Using Print Punctuation   44
Using Print Symbols   48
Using Print Emphasis   51
Using Print Spaces   52
Using Print Paragraphs   53
Using Print Vertical Spacing   54

4   Formatting Your Text   55

Choosing Your Fonts   56
Choosing Your Font Size   59
Choosing Your Vertical Spacing   60
Controlling Horizontal Spacing   61
Controlling Justification   63
Controlling Hyphenation   64
Controlling Page Endings   65

**Working with Word #4:
Using Styles**   **66**

5   Perfecting Your Text   71

Fixing Letterspacing   72
Fixing Line Endings   73
Fixing Paragraphs   75
Fixing Page Endings   77

6   Handling Special Text   79

   Handling Lists   80
   Handling Headers and Footers   81
   Handling Page Numbering   83
   Handling Footnotes and Endnotes   84
   Handling Automated Text   85
   Handling Indexes   87

7   Handling Graphics   95

   Preparing Graphics   96
   Placing Graphics   100

8   Enhancing Your Layout   105

   Adding Tables   106
   Adding Text Boxes and Frames   107
   Adding Borders and Backgrounds   109
   Adding Ornaments   111

   Working with Word #5:
      Using Alignment Aids   **112**

9   Preparing for Print   113

   Choosing a Print Service   114
   Centering Your Pages   115
   Preparing Hard Copy   117
   Preparing Word Files   118
   Preparing PDF Files   119
   Placing Crop Marks   128
   Checking Your Work   130

10 Creating a Cover   131

Setting Your Cover Size   132
Setting Your Cover Margins   134
Handling Cover Type   136
Handling Cover Graphics   138
Adding a Bar Code   139
Preparing Your Cover for Print   140
Checking Your Cover   143

Resources   145

Books   146
Web Sites   148
Newsgroups   149
Email Discussion Lists   150
Newsletters   151

Index   153

About This Book

Nowadays, new technologies and services have made it easier than ever to publish your book. But if you mean to design it yourself, you may face an important question: Do I need an expensive page layout program like Adobe InDesign, Adobe PageMaker, or QuarkXPress? Or can I instead use a word processor like Microsoft Word?

Ask an old-style publishing professional, and you will most likely be told that you need a page layout program. Yet many upstart and even established publishers use Word instead. Most of my own books have been produced in Word— including this one.

It's true that Word lacks some advanced typographic features found in page layout programs. But if you know the basic principles of typography and book design and how to apply them, there's no reason a book you produce in Word should look less than professional. And if you *don't* know those principles, then a page layout program won't help you!

Besides that, a word processor can actually be the better choice for some books. Page layout programs excel at composing pages with substantial graphics and sophisticated layout, such as for magazines or textbooks. But they can be clumsy when handling long and complex text—which is just what Word does well.

Also, use of a page layout program makes more sense when the book designer is someone other than the author. For an author-designer-publisher, using one program for both writing and layout can simplify and speed your work. This is especially true if your book will need revisions or updates. A program like Word can automatically adjust for text additions and deletions in such a way that little or no manual reformatting is required.

Word is seldom surpassed in its abilities to create automatic tables of contents, indexes, and cross-references. It's also excellent in its automatic handling of footnotes and endnotes—something a page layout program might not even attempt.

Finally, some publishers who have tried both Word and a page layout program will tell you that the page layout program may produce slightly better text, but that Word can more than make up for it with easier, speedier formatting.

In the past, one good reason to avoid Word for publishing was that its printer files played well only with desktop printers, not with printing presses. But Adobe Acrobat and its Portable Document Format (PDF) have changed that. Today's digital presses easily handle PDF files created by Acrobat and other programs from Word documents.

In this book, I'll tell you how to produce pages that no book reviewer will scoff at, and I'll offer other helpful tips as well on using Word. But, no, I will not tell you everything you'll need to know. If you're publishing with Word, you'll definitely want a good, comprehensive manual on your version.

I also highly recommend that you get and read a copy of James Felici's *The Complete Manual of Typography*. In fact, that might be the most important tip you find here! Though I've done my best to give you the basics of book design and typography, Felici will give you many of the details.

You'll also want to look at a multitude of commercially published books for examples of typography and book design. See what works—and what doesn't! And while you probably won't want to exactly duplicate an existing book design, there's nothing wrong with using elements that appeal to you.

This version of my book is based on Word 97–2003 for Windows, and on Word 2004 for the Mac.* Word's typographic features do not change often, but its interface does—and Word 2007 will bring the biggest changes in over a decade. If you're on a Word version that doesn't show a command or setting where I say it is, please use Word's Help function or your manual to find what you need. And if you discover an additional way to do something, consider it a bonus!

Though I can't offer private technical assistance for Word, I welcome your feedback to help me improve future editions. Please bring your comments and suggestions to my Publishing Page at

www.aaronshep.com/publishing

While you're there, check for updates to this book, including notes on Word 2007 and 2008. And be sure to sign up for my email bulletin so I can let you know about further online updates and new editions.

---

* If you're still on Mac OS 9 and need to use Word 98 or 2001, visit me at www.aaronshep.com/publishing and ask for a free copy of my earlier ebook *Books, Typography, and Microsoft Word.*

Working with Word #1: Choosing A Version

Not all Word versions are created equal.

On Windows, Word 97 was considered a huge leap forward from previous versions, so anything earlier should be avoided. Between that version and Word 2003, the program hasn't changed much typographically, but Word 2000 and Word 2003 are considered more stable and better behaved. Of those two, many Word experts prefer Word 2000, feeling that the latter version added features and complexity without really becoming more useful. But of course, the latter version also stands to be supported longer by Microsoft.

On the Mac side, the picture has been different. Negative reaction to Word 6 for the Mac prompted Microsoft to spin off development of the Mac version. The result was that Word for the Mac lagged typographically behind its Windows sibling for almost a decade. Only with Word 2004 has it almost caught back up. So, if you're using any earlier Mac version, I advise you to upgrade. One hitch is that Word 2004 mishandles black-and-white graphics—by design, not by error. (I describe workarounds for this problem.)

On Mac OS 9, Word 98 is a more reliable choice than Word 2001, which is prone to corrupting its settings files.

And what about Word 2007 for Windows and Word 2008 for the Mac? This book was published before they appeared—so check my Publishing Page for my comments on them.

www.aaronshep.com/publishing

1
Managing Word

Microsoft Word can be stodgy, stuttering, and treacherous. It can also be speedy and reliable. It depends a lot on how you use it.

Managing Updates

New versions of Word are not really finished when first sold. They only start working properly after the first major update or two. So, the *first* thing to do after installing Word is to check on the Microsoft Web site for updates, and install whatever you find. Then check again every month or so. Luckily, current versions of Word make this very easy. Just choose "Check for Updates" from the Help menu.

The corollary of all this is that you should wait till at least the first update before adopting any new major version of Word!

Managing Options or Preferences

On the various tabs of the Options dialog box (Windows) or the Preferences dialog box (Mac), Word includes numerous settings that affect the program's speed, efficiency, convenience, and reliability. Some of the most important ones are among the most obscure. Here are my recommendations for various tabs. (Not all choices will appear in all Word versions.)

General. In later versions of Word for Windows, turn off "Automatically create drawing canvas when inserting Auto-Shapes." Unless you're producing complex drawings in Word, the Drawing Canvas is more confusing than helpful.

In later versions of Word for the Mac, you might want to turn off "WYSIWYG font and style menus." This will let Word start up much faster.

Security. Turn on macro virus protection, or set the level to Medium or higher. In earlier versions of Word, this setting is on the General tab.

Save. Turn *off* "Allow fast saves," and also "Allow background saves," if you have it. The Fast Saves feature is considered the single biggest cause of Word file corruption, and background saves too can be risky, because your computer is handling more than one task at once. At the same time, neither feature significantly increases the speed of file saving.

Turn on "Save AutoRecover info" and set it for at least every five minutes. This will help you recover work in case of a program or system crash. But don't confuse this with an automatic save feature! You still need to save your work manually.

Edit. Turn off "Keep track of formatting," if you have it. This will help prevent file bloat and clutter and will also keep your styles listing clean.

Turn on "Use smart cut and paste." This is very helpful in adding or subtracting spaces as needed between words and sentences. (Watch out, though, because it sometimes inserts an unwanted space at the start of a paragraph.) In later versions, this feature has been enhanced with additional optional functions. I suggest keeping the default settings, but reviewing them if Word isn't acting as you'd like.

Turn off "When selecting, automatically select entire word," since this keeps you from selecting only part of a word. Also turn off "Use smart paragraph selection" or "Include paragraph mark when selecting paragraphs," two wordings for the same setting. This one is dangerous, because the paragraph mark contains the paragraph's formatting! You want full control over whether or not it's selected.

Spelling and Grammar. Turn off "Check spelling as you type." Instead, use the Spelling and Grammar command as needed. This can speed up Word.

View. Turn off "Wrap to window" and "Draft Font." This will make sure that Normal View displays your text lines as they'll appear in print.

In Word for the Mac—at least on slower machines—turn off "Live Word Count." Instead, use the Word Count command on the Tools menu as needed.

Print. In Windows, turn off "Draft output."

On the Mac, the once essential "Fractional Widths" option seems to have no function in Word 2004.

Compatibility. First turn *off* every option by choosing your current Word version from the pull-down menu. These options are offered primarily to let you print documents from earlier versions and from other programs without producing layout changes in the printed output—but they can be the cause of subtle and not-so-subtle problems. Clearing the options lets Word work as it was designed to, with all the improvements made to it over the years. In general, you do *not* want Word to adopt obsolete or foreign behaviors.

But there are at least two exceptions. Turn *on* "Do full justification like WordPerfect 6.x for Windows" and "Don't use HTML paragraph auto spacing." I'll discuss these settings in more detail later, but basically, the first improves the quality of justification, and the second stops Word from overlapping Spacing Before and After.

Especially make sure this one is *off:* "Use printer metrics to lay out document." If this is on, the layout of your document can change every time you switch desktop printers, or even when you update a printer driver! With the option off, Word strictly controls printed layout according to its own internal data, keeping that layout consistent no matter how the document is printed.

The only case in which you *might* want the printer metrics option on would be if your printing service was taking Word files directly instead of PDF. I discuss how that might work in my chapter on preparing for print—but I don't recommend sending Word files!

Note that all these Compatibility settings apply *only to the document you're working on*—unless you end by clicking the "Default" button, which applies them to the active template. But even if you do, old documents must still be changed one at a time.

Managing the Workspace

Do you find Office Assistant as annoying as I do? In Windows, exorcise it by changing Word's or Office's configuration in the Add or Remove Programs control panel. On the Mac, the best way is to find the Office Assistant folder within your Word or Office folder and yank it to the Trash. And don't worry, you can still get assistance from the Help menu.

Some Word versions show only a selection of the commands on a menu or toolbar unless you click on arrows to display more. This is supposed to simplify things, but it can be confusing and make it harder to find the commands. To see all commands, click the Options tab in the Customize dialog box and select "Always show full menus" and "Show Standard and Formatting toolbars on two rows."

Each of Word's many available toolbars can turned on or off from the View menu. And if they don't appear where you'd like them, just move them by clicking and dragging on their left end. Make them float close to where you need them, or dock them at another edge. On the Mac, you can even reshape them by dragging the lower right corner.

In Word for the Mac, you can prevent the Formatting Palette from fading away by turning this off in the Customize Formatting Palette dialog box.

For people who prefer leaving their hands on the keyboard instead of reaching for the mouse, Word has a huge number of key combinations for commands, insertions, and cursor movements. To see a complete list, search for "Keyboard Shortcuts" in Word's Help.

Word is also infinitely customizable, so feel free to make it fit your specific way of working. Using the Customize dialog box, you can modify Word's toolbars and menus or create your own. You can make them include commands that otherwise take several steps to access, or even "hidden" Word commands not normally available at all. And anything that can be assigned to a toolbar button or menu item can be assigned to a keyboard shortcut as well.

One piece of advice, though: It's best to create your own toolbars and menus instead of modifying Word's. That will simplify things if and when you move to a later version, because Word's changes won't be mixed up with yours.

Managing Automatic Changes

By default, Word watches over your work and automatically makes certain changes based on what Microsoft *thinks* you want. While some such changes are helpful, others can be maddening. They can even cause errors, if you don't notice what happened.

Later versions of Word have added AutoCorrect Options buttons that appear when some changes are made. These let you reverse the changes and even prevent future ones. To stop such changes when using older versions—or if you just want to stop the changes ahead of time—choose "AutoCorrect" or "AutoCorrect Options" from the Tools menu. In the dialog box, click on the tabs for "AutoCorrect" and "AutoFormat As You Type" and uncheck anything you'd rather do without.

There are two options you almost certainly want to keep, though, that are on the "AutoFormat As You Type" tab: "Replace straight quotes with smart quotes," and if you have it, "Replace fractions with fraction character." (Word 2004 for the Mac does replace fractions but neglects to list this function in the settings.) I discuss these in my chapter on typesetting.

While you're in the AutoCorrect dialog box, you can also click on the AutoText tab and choose whether to keep "AutoComplete." Personally, I consider this feature mainly a distraction for someone who types with reasonable speed and accuracy.

Managing Features

Sometimes Word can't handle the complexity of its own "advanced" features, which leads to file corruption. And even if these features don't corrupt your file, they may still lead to file bloat. Here is a list of those I recommend staying away from, or turning off if you've been using them.

• Master Documents. This feature is considered a sure path to file corruption.

• Track Changes.

• Versions.

• Automatic list numbering and bulleting, especially if applied apart from a style.

If you're turning off any of these functions, follow up with a "Save As" to clean the file.

Luckily, none of these features is essential. You don't need Master Documents, because Word is efficient enough to keep the text of an entire book in a single file. And instead of saving versions and tracking changes in one file, it's easy enough to save a series of numbered or dated files for reference. I also like to keep a document "Out" file where I paste significant pieces of text I'm removing, in case I want to retrieve them later without hunting through old versions.

Managing Old Files

In this chapter, I've given a lot of advice on protecting and optimizing your documents. This is all good for *new* ones, but what about those already compromised? Here's how to clean them up.

1. First make sure you've turned *off* "Allow Fast Saves," and "Keep track of formatting" if you have it, in your Options or Preferences.

2. Open your document and turn off or remove any of the harmful "advanced" features I mentioned.

3. Set your Compatibility Options or Preferences as described.

4. Finally, from the File menu, do a "Save As" rather than a simple "Save." Be sure the chosen format is your current Word version's default, which will probably be named "Word Document." Leave the filename and location as is. This will replace the old file with a new one, completely rewritten and in much better shape.

Follow the same steps with all the Word templates you've been using, again choosing the default format, which will probably be "Document Template." If you don't know where your templates are, look in your File Locations Options or Preferences. (For more on location, see the following section.)

If a document is already acting strangely due to possible corruption, you can sometimes fix it by saving it in another format—say, XML, or a Web page, or Word 2, or even as text—then importing it back into your current version and restoring any lost formatting. Or try copying and pasting everything *except* the final paragraph mark into a new document. Or try deleting all section breaks and inserting new ones.

Managing Safety

While working in Word, be sure to follow the usual rules of safe computing. Save your work every few minutes and make regular, rotating backups at varying intervals, with at least some backups to drives or media outside your computer.

It's just as important to back up your custom settings files as it is to back up your documents—or more so. Word for Windows doesn't make it easy, though. These files—including your own templates, by default—are located in invisible folders.

To access these files more easily, you can tell Windows to show invisible files and folders. This is done on the View tab of the Folder Options control panel. In recent versions of Word, you can then find the general Word settings file in

C:\Documents and Settings\[UserName]\
Application Data\Microsoft\Office\

The templates are in

C:\Documents and Settings\[UserName]\
Application Data\Microsoft\Templates\

If you like, you can move all your templates somewhere that's more accessible for backup. Then just go to Word's File Locations Options to tell Word where to find them.

On the Mac, you don't need to deal with invisibility. In recent versions, to find the default location for custom templates, go to the application's folder, then the Templates folder, then My Templates. On the Mac too, this location can be changed in Word Preferences. For other Word settings files, go to your user folder, then Library, then Preferences.

Use a UPS (uninterrupted power supply) in case of power failure. The surest way to lose a file—and perhaps your entire system—is to let the power go out while a file is being saved.

Of course, Windows users should have a good antivirus program—and keep it updated! (On the Mac too, this may someday be necessary—but at this writing, it still isn't.)

Avoid possible crashes by restarting the program at the first sign of any slowdown or odd behavior. In fact, even if there's no trouble, you should shut down Word entirely now and then—say, once in the middle of the day and again at the end—so the program can reset itself.

Managing Memory

Word likes to load as much of a document as possible into memory so it can display any part without accessing your hard drive. This makes for very fast navigation. But if the file is too large for available memory, Word can't do this.

This trouble may be caused especially by numbers of high-resolution or color graphics. As I discuss in my chapter on graphics, there are a number of strategies for reducing the load, including linking to graphics instead of embedding them.

But if Word is slow or prone to crashing, the best solution is sometimes just to add memory to your computer. If you've never added any, you should probably at least double what you have, since computers are seldom sold with enough. Specific needs will vary, but 512 MB is generally a minimum for text and light graphics, and 1 GB for text with heavy graphics. It doesn't hurt to double those figures, and in any case, the minimums will likely increase with future updates of Word and your operating system.

Working with Word #2: Using Views

Word has a number of ways to help you see better what you and the program are doing. To start with, resize your window and set the Zoom so that the type size and line length on screen are comfortable for reading. (If you're on an LCD monitor, first make sure your display is at the monitor's highest resolution, or your text won't display clearly.)

You can see your document in several different views. The two basic ones for editing and formatting are Normal View, which presents the document in a continuous scroll, and Print Layout View (Windows) or Page Layout View (Mac), which shows you roughly what a printed page will look like, including headers and footers.

Though choosing between the two views is largely a matter of preference, Normal View can be more efficient for working with straight text and inline graphics. It is often faster than Print or Page Layout View, and you can see the text in an uninterrupted flow. On the other hand, you'll need Print or Page Layout View when you work with headers and footers, floating graphics, text boxes, or other elements that don't show up in Normal View.

To make formatting easier in Normal View, make sure it displays your text lines as they'll appear in print. To do this, check your View Options and make sure "Wrap to window" and "Draft font" are *off*.

Print Preview—and don't confuse this with Print Layout View—gives you Word's best picture of how your document will look in print. If you zoom in far enough, you can even get a fairly accurate view of the spacings between words and letters.

Print Preview also lets you view facing pages together. Set this up with the Multiple Pages button on the Print Preview toolbar, or just zoom out. If your document's paper size matches your final book size, you'll see your pages just as they should appear in your bound and open book. To get the pages paired correctly, though—with odd pages on the right—you'll need to set up your document for "Different odd and even" headers and footers, as explained in my chapter on formatting your document.

Also useful for books is Outline View. This lets you view just your headings, giving an overview of your book's structure. Just click on the number on the Outlining toolbar that represents the lowest heading level you want to include. (Outline View is safer than Word's newer Document Map, which can change the style of some paragraphs without warning.)

In Outline View, you can move chapters and other large divisions by just dragging the symbols to the left of the headings. You can also use this view to quickly navigate your book by placing your cursor on the heading closest to your destination and switching back to your usual view.

There are times when you need to work with more than one spot in your document at once. Word lets you divide the editing window into two completely functional parts. Just select "Split" from the Window menu, or drag the split box at the top of the vertical scroll bar. Or use the New Window command to create one or more additional windows for showing your document. Each pane or window can be in its own view, too—Normal, Print or Page Layout, Outline, whatever you like.

When formatting your document, it's most helpful to be able to see formatting marks that are normally invisible, such as spaces, tab characters, Optional Hyphens, and paragraph marks. The paragraph mark is especially important because that's where Word stores all of the paragraph's formatting. If you accidentally delete the mark, the formatting goes with it.

The simplest way to make these symbols visible is to click "Show/Hide"—the button with the paragraph mark, ¶—on the main toolbar, or select "Show All" from the View menu. This also allows you to see page breaks and section breaks in Print or Page Layout View, as you do in Normal View. For more control, though, you can go to your View Options or Preferences and select visibility for individual elements.

At times, you'll want to find out every bit of formatting applied to specific text. If you're on a later version of Word for Windows, the best way to do this is to select the text or just place your cursor within it and call up the Reveal Formatting task pane. Or for any version, you can choose "What's This?" from the Help menu (Windows) or "Reveal Formatting" from the View menu (Mac), then click on the text. To return to normal, choose the command again or press the Esc key.

2

Formatting Your Document

If you try to treat Word like a page layout program or a type-writer, you're more than likely to be frustrated. But if you learn Word's own ways of working, it can be an efficient tool for setting up your book.

Setting Up Your File

Actually, what I want to tell you here is how *not* to set up your document. In general, you *don't* want to separate the text of your book into multiple files.

Word's files can be surprisingly compact—much more so than the files of a page layout program—and in most cases you can fit an entire book comfortably in a single file with no loss of editing speed. If you have a number of high-resolution graphics, you might want to keep those in separate files, as explained in my chapter on graphics—but for the text itself, one file does fine.

Whatever you do, *don't* use Word's Master Documents feature. This is supposed to allow you to handle collectively a group of book text files in imitation of page layout programs. Unfortunately, it is considered an almost sure path to document corruption. Even if you do split your book into numerous text files, be sure to avoid Master Documents.

Setting Your Page Size

The first and most basic decision you'll make on the design of your book is the size of your page. In publishing, this is called the *trim size,* because it's the size of the book pages after excess paper has been trimmed away.

Your print service will likely have a set of preferred trim sizes it handles. The most common size for U.S. *trade books*—books designed mostly for bookstores—is 6 × 9 inches. You can count on this size being offered by almost any U.S. print service. Other common U.S. sizes include 5½ × 8½, 7 × 10, and 8½ × 11. (In the U.S., width is always given before height, and I follow that here unless otherwise stated. A book described as 9 × 6 inches, then, would be wider than it is tall.)

In the U.K., common sizes in millimeters—with height given before width—are 216 × 138 (Demy), 234 × 156 (Royal), 246 × 189 (Crown), and 297 × 210 (A4).

There are a couple of ways to handle these different page sizes in Word. One way is to center the content of your pages on the standard 8½ × 11 or A4 sheet. Some print services actually request this for your PDF files, and some publishers prefer to work like that anyway—so I'll tell you how to do it in my chapter on preparing for print.

For now, though, the best idea is to set the *paper size* in your Word document to equal your book's final trim size. In other words, if your book pages are 6 × 9, you tell Word to compose the pages on a sheet just that big. This way, you'll have the choice of creating a PDF file with pages at exactly trim size. Also, Word will show your pages on screen just as they'll appear in the book, which makes checking your margins and overall layout much easier.

In Word, paper size is set in the Page Setup dialog box, on the Paper or Paper Size tab or pull-down menu. In Windows, you can enter the settings for any paper size you like.

On the Mac, it's a bit more complex. If your desired size isn't listed on the system's pull-down menu, you can add it there with any program that enables such customizing. This includes Acrobat and most other Adobe programs. Word itself adds a Custom Paper Size panel to the Mac's Page Setup, and you can use this in a pinch. But it works only for viewing on screen, not for creating PDF files at trim size.

If you're setting the paper size for an existing document instead of a new one, be sure to do a "Select All" before opening the dialog box, or the change may not apply throughout.

Note that you're not setting up your pages in "spreads" or figuring out in what order your pages will be printed. Unless you're printing and binding books at home, leave all that to your printing service. Just set up your document for one page at a time, from first to last. (You can always check your spreads in Print Preview—but if you need them visible while you work, you'll need a page layout program.)

By the way, if you're using print on demand, you probably won't be able to publish books with horizontal, or "landscape," orientation—books wider than they are tall. Most POD operations support only vertical, or "portrait," orientation because of the limitations of their binding methods.

Setting Your Page Margins

On a typewriter, you set left and right margins by moving stops on a ruler. In a page layout program, you generally draw a box to contain the text, then create additional pages, each with a box connected to the one before.

Word offers both ruler stops and text boxes, but neither one of these is the appropriate way to set your document's margins. Instead, go to the dialog box for Page Setup (Windows) or Document Format (Mac). There you'll set the left, right, top, and bottom margins of your text block.

Then what are Word's ruler stops for? They're mostly for such tasks as setting indents on the first or subsequent lines of paragraphs, or occasionally indenting an entire paragraph for block quoting. In other words, they're for positioning text in relation to the margins you've already set. (You can also perform these tasks in the Paragraph Format dialog box.)

There are many factors that go into deciding how wide to set the margins of your book page—the page size, your font and its readability, whether you want to reduce the number of pages or increase them, and pure aesthetics. For a 6 × 9 or 5½ × 8½ inch book, you'll probably want to stick with side margins between ½ and 1 inch, and vertical margins between ¾ and 1¼ inches.

Keep in mind that you have to allow for inexact trimming! Also, if your book will be printed on large sheets, you might have to deal with text "creeping" sideways from one page to the next after the sheet is folded and trimmed. But this should not be a problem with modern equipment or print on demand.

Some designers like to shift their page content toward the outer edge of the book, or the inside edge—the *gutter*. Personally, with the vagaries of trimming, I find it simpler and safer to leave the content centered, with equal margins left and right. But if you do want to shift it, you can set unequal margin sizes and select "Mirror margins."

Some binding methods—like comb binding—take up a substantial chunk of the inside edge. In this case, you can set mirrored margins or just enter a measurement for "Gutter."

Along with the other margin settings, you'll find settings for header and footer margins, either on the same tab or on the Layout tab. These regulate the distance of the headers and footers from the top and bottom edges of the page. (Don't confuse *headers* with *headings,* which are elements like titles that identify the text that follows them.)

Since headers and footers appear outside the main text area, the header margin must be smaller than the top margin, and the footer margin must be smaller than the bottom one. For instance, if you have a bottom margin of 1 inch, you could set the footer margin to ½ inch, making the footer sit at that distance from the page's bottom edge. If you add a second line to the footer—even a blank one—the *second* line will sit at ½ inch from the bottom edge, pushing the first line up.

Generally, you want your main text area either centered vertically on the page, or else slightly raised, with the bottom margin larger than the top. Headers and footers should be a safe distance from the page edge—say, at least ½ inch—but far enough from the main text that they're clearly separate from it.

Sometimes you might want to extend past your side margins—for instance, if you have a table or graphic a little wider than your text lines. You can use the ruler for this too, after selecting your element or putting your cursor in it. On the right, you can just drag the ruler stop. On the left, first bring this part of the ruler into view by pressing the Shift key while scrolling sideways. You can also just enter a negative number for indenting in the Paragraph Format dialog box.

Setting Up Sections

Look at a number of commercially published books to get a feel for the various parts of a book, their sequence, and their positioning. For instance, many major elements should appear or start only on a right-hand, odd page, even if it means leaving the left-hand page blank. Such elements include the title page, the table of contents, a preface or introduction, and pages starting numbered parts (Part 1, Part 2, and so on). They also include one or more chapters—always the first chapter of the book, usually the first chapter of each numbered part, and traditionally, *all* chapters—though this is no longer common. The copyright page—the page with copyright and other bibliographic info—nearly always appears as the left-hand page that immediately follows the title page. Also notice that headers and footers may change depending on where they are.

For a complete rundown of book elements, see a style guide such as *The Chicago Manual of Style*—a standard reference in the publishing industry—or a self-publishing manual such as Jennifer Basye Sander's excellent *The Complete Idiot's Guide to Self-Publishing*.

With Word, you're probably used to inserting a page break whenever you want to start a new page. But what if starting a chapter on an odd page means *skipping* a page? Do you insert two page breaks?

That doesn't work well for several reasons. First, if text editing later adds or subtracts a page before that, your chapter will start on an even page. Also, a blank page before the chapter should be *completely* blank, with no header or footer, and inserting page breaks won't give you that. Finally, dividing chapters only by page breaks gives you no convenient way to vary headers and footers.

But Word has a solution to these problems: the section break. By inserting section breaks that will separate chapters and other book parts, you can choose to start them either on the very next page or on an odd or an even one. If this means skipping a page, Word will omit any header or footer on the skipped page so it's completely blank. Section breaks also let you give each book part its own set of headers and footers.

Best of all, these section breaks move with the text. If you add one or more pages anywhere in your book, everything that comes after will shift automatically. You don't have to change a thing.

Word's section breaks, by the way, are one of its most important advantages over page layout programs. InDesign, for example, allows you to define sections to control headers and footers. But blank pages must be inserted manually, and if you add a page anywhere, all following section breaks must be manually adjusted. Though InDesign beats Word at managing books kept in multiple files, it is much less efficient for working with those in a single one.

To insert a section break, choose "Break" from the Insert menu. From the dialog box or submenu, select from among section breaks for a "next," "even," or "odd" page. To later change a section's starting page, place your cursor anywhere in the section and select "Page Setup" from the File menu (Windows) or "Document" from the Format menu (Mac). Then click the Layout tab and look for the "Section start" setting.

Though Word's sections are a powerful feature, dealing with them can be tricky. Be aware that many page and document formatting changes will apply by default only to the section that holds the cursor. To format your entire document, first select all of it, or else use the appropriate drop-down menu that lets you specify what sections the change applies to. In the Mac's Page Setup dialog box, this menu is on the separate

"Microsoft Word" panel, even though it affects all Page Setup changes!

Also keep in mind that a section's properties are stored *not* at its beginning but in the section break at its *end*—or in the case of the last section, in the final paragraph mark. In other words, a section break doesn't really tell Word how to format the *following* section. Instead, it tells Word to *stop* applying the formatting of the *previous* section and to get new properties from the *next* section break. (Sure, the section break you see before a chapter in Normal View says "Odd Page" or whatever you chose—but that's just to confuse you!)

So, what if you have each chapter in its own section and you want to move one chapter to a different position, along with its own headers and footers? What you *don't* want to do is include the section break that comes before the chapter. Instead, select and move the chapter plus the break at its *end*. (You'll need to be in Normal View to see the breaks.)

What if you want to remove a section break to merge two sections? Let's say again that you have each chapter in its own section. If you delete the break between chapters 1 and 2, then both chapters will have the section properties of Chapter 2.

But what if you want both chapters to have the section properties of Chapter 1? For that, you must replace the break after Chapter 2 with the break after Chapter 1. First cut the break between the chapters, then paste it back just above the break that follows Chapter 2. Then delete that other break.

As an alternate method, you can copy all of Chapter 1's section formatting to Chapter 2 before removing the break. Here's the simplest way: Place your cursor in Chapter 1, open the dialog box for Page Setup (Windows) or Document Format (Mac), and click OK without changing anything. Then place your cursor in Chapter 2 and use the Repeat Typing command.

You'll need this method, for instance, if your second section falls at the end of your document, without a break following it.

Be aware that, because Word packs so much formatting data into its section breaks, they are particularly prone to corruption. If you have an especially stubborn formatting or printing problem, the only solution may be to delete one or more section breaks and insert fresh ones. And for an especially complex document, when you expect to be pushing the pieces around quite a bit, you might even wait and insert section breaks as one of your final steps.

Setting Up Headers and Footers

Headers are repeating lines that appear at the tops of pages. (Don't confuse them with *headings* like titles.) *Footers* are repeating lines that appear at page bottoms.

If you look at commercially published books, you'll see that the use and design of headers and footers can vary widely. Nearly always, they identify the book title and page number, but they can also identify the chapter or the author. Often there is different information on odd and even pages—or even if the information is the same, the placement may be mirrored.

Individual pages can include a header, a footer, or both, or neither. Often a chapter will have a header on each page except the first, which may instead have a footer with the page number only—or no header or footer at all. And of course, a page with no text should never have any header, footer, or page number.

Word with its section breaks offers complete control over all of this, plus automatic placement that is so convenient that users of some page layout programs might envy it.

For each section, Word's settings allow you to have different headers and footers for even and odd pages, plus a different header and footer (or none) for the section's first page. You can change these settings on the Layout tab of the dialog box for Page Setup (Windows) or Document Format (Mac) whenever your cursor is in the right section.

I'll discuss editing headers and footers later, in my chapter on handling special text.

Setting Up Columns

There are several ways to set up columns in Word. You could set them up as a table, as you would on a Web page. Or you could draw text boxes, as you would in a page layout program. But the best way is also the simplest. Just choose "Columns" from the Format menu, enter a few settings, and you're done!

Well, maybe it's not *quite* that simple, because you have to make sure you're formatting what you intend. If you just place your cursor somewhere in a section, the entire section will be changed to columns—or the entire document, if it's not divided. If that's not what you want, insert section breaks before and after. If these breaks are "Continuous," then your columns can appear right on the same page with other text.

A slightly different way to set up columns is to enter and select text before choosing the "Columns" command. Word then inserts section breaks before and after as needed.

One advantage of using the Columns feature instead of a table is that text will flow automatically from one column to the next. Normally, this will happen when text reaches the bottom of a page, but you can make it happen earlier by inserting a column break. Or insert a "Continuous" section break after the columns to make Word even them up automatically.

To get rid of columns, just place your cursor in that section, again use the Columns command, and select "One."

In Normal View, column text shows only as a single narrow column, but you can see it properly both in Print or Page Layout View and in Print Preview.

Working with Word #3: Using Templates

Every document in Word is based on one or more *templates*. When you create a new document, Word simply makes a copy of one of these templates, which you then edit and save as a regular document under a new name. These templates start with default settings and formatting, but you can customize them any way you like—right down to altering the menus and toolbars that Word displays.

Word includes templates for many types of documents. One template is especially important: Normal.dot—or Normal, as it might appear on the Mac—also known as the Blank Document template. If you just open a new document without specifying a special kind, this is the template it will come from. But *every* document draws from its resources, even if the document is based on another template.

For instance, if you create a document from a template called CerealBox, the document will include all of CerealBox's styles. But it will also include all styles from the Blank Document template—as long as they don't conflict with CerealBox's.

By the way, if you ever want to start fresh with the Normal or Normal.dot file, you don't have to reinstall it. Just delete it from your computer and Word will replace it automatically.

It's easy to create your own template from scratch by customizing a document and doing a "Save As" in the Document Template format. And if you're producing a number of books in a similar style, you'll probably find it worthwhile to create a special "Book" template, with all your custom settings, styles, layout, and standardized content in place.

Though you could instead simply duplicate an old book file to create a new one, a template is the handiest place to store refinements over time. You can then instantly update all of a document's styles from the template with Word's Style Gallery, or just specific styles with the Organizer.

Many of Word's dialog boxes include options to make the changes also in the document's template, or to make the settings the "default," which is saying the same thing. You can also open the template file itself in Word and make changes directly. To find the location of these files for your version and platform, check Word's File Locations Options or Preferences, or see Word's Help.

If you customize your templates at all, you're going to want to back them up just as you do your documents. If they're not in a convenient location for that, you can move them wherever you like, then tell Word where to find them in the File Locations Options or Preferences.

If you retain your custom templates when updating to a new major version of Word, be sure to open each template and "Save As." You won't need to change the name, location, or format. This will bring it up to date for the new version.

For the Normal template, though, it's better to keep the new one Word installs and use the Organizer to transfer custom elements from your old one. Using an outdated Normal template can cause problems that are very hard to pin down.

Some Word experts advise against storing customizations in the Normal template at all, since its constant use makes it particularly prone to corruption. Instead, they tell you to set up a separate template for all general customizations, then put it in Word's Startup directory or folder to activate automatically whenever you start Word.

3
Typesetting Your Text

Despite all the power in a modern word processor, many people still use them largely like typewriters—even if those people have never touched a typewriter! Here are some important differences between typewriter text and text for print.

Using Print Punctuation

One of the surest signs of the publishing amateur—and unfortunately a sign seen more and more often—is the use of typewriter punctuation in place of punctuation meant for print. The keyboard designed for the typewriter and largely inherited by the computer simply doesn't include all the punctuation marks needed for print typography, and its intended substitutes look completely out of place in books.

Chief among the culprits are "straight" quotes and apostrophes. Only "curly" quotes and apostrophes should appear in a book.

" '   " ' ' "

Wrong   Right

In Word, curly quotes can be inserted with special key combinations, or with the Symbol command on the Insert menu—but the simplest way is with Word's AutoFormat.

Choose "AutoCorrect" from the Tools menu, click the AutoFormat tab, and make sure the "smart quotes" option is selected. Then click the "AutoFormat As You Type" tab and do the same there. Now the straight characters you type will be curled automatically. And if the document has straight characters from before—or if any are pasted in later—you can curl them all together by selecting "AutoFormat" from the Format menu.

Another way to curl characters throughout a document is with the Replace All command, putting the same straight character in both fields. With the smart quotes options on, the characters will be curled as they replace.

With AutoFormat, a character will sometimes curl the wrong way—for instance, after a dash in some cases, or before a word such as *'tis* that's contracted at the beginning. If this happens, just add a space or a letter in front, type the character, then delete the extra.

'Tis   'Tis

Wrong   Right

Hyphens, single or paired, should never take the place of true dashes, or *em dashes,* as they're properly called. By default, when you type two hyphens, Word will replace them with a dash as part of its "AutoFormat As You Type" feature. You can also insert one manually from the Symbol dialog box or with a special key combination—Alt-Control-Minus (on the numeric keypad) in Windows, Shift-Option-Hyphen or Command-Option-Minus on the Mac. Note that the em dash should *not* have a space before or after.

a -- a   a — a   a—a

Wrong   Wrong   Right

There is one more dash that's good to use: the *en dash.* In length, this is partway between a hyphen and an em dash. It's used to convey a range, as in "2004–2007" or "pages 2–11" or "May–August." You can't use AutoFormat for this one, but you can still insert it from the Symbol dialog box or with a special key combination—Control-Minus (on the numeric keypad) in Windows, Option-Hyphen or Command-Minus on the Mac. While most readers won't notice the difference between an en dash and a hyphen, it's a nice touch for those who will.

Oddly, one of the punctuation marks available on the computer actually works less well than the typewriter equivalent. That's the *ellipsis,* the series of three dots that signifies a lapse in text.

On the typewriter, the way to insert an ellipsis is to type three periods in a row. This looks about right because the typeface is monospace, making the periods seem spread out. But when you do the same on the computer in a proportional font, the three periods are much too close together.

Yes, the computer offers an ellipsis as a single character of three dots. You can enter it from the Symbol dialog box; or with the AutoCorrect feature; or with Alt-Control-Period (Windows) or Option-Semicolon (Mac). But for some odd reason, this character is always made to look about the same as three periods typed together, still without the needed space between.

For this reason, professional typographers ignore the computer ellipsis entirely and build their own, with spaces between the periods, as well as before and after.

a...a   a . . . a

Wrong   Right

Various kinds of spaces can be used to separate the periods, but in Word, the best choice is the Nonbreaking Space. This space won't be altered by line justification and won't let the ellipsis break in two at the end of a line. Insert this space from the Symbol dialog box; or with Control-Shift-Space (Windows) or Option-Space (Mac). In most cases, the spaces before and after the ellipsis should be normal ones.

Sometimes a period and an ellipsis will appear together so that you see four dots—but the period and the ellipsis are still separate marks, so the spacing will depend on the situation. If the lapse in text occurs *between* sentences, then the ellipsis comes after the period, with a normal space between. If the lapse itself *ends* a sentence, then the ellipsis is followed by a Nonbreaking Space and then the period.

Using Print Symbols

Many useful symbols not seen on a typewriter are stashed away in computer fonts, and especially in the Unicode fonts now supplied with Word and current operating systems. In Word for Windows, you can access all these characters in the Symbol dialog box. Later versions also let you enter a Unicode character directly into your text by typing its numeric code then pressing Alt-X. (See Word Help for entering a more limited set of symbols by ASCII code.)

On the Mac, you can use Word's dialog box for many symbols, but many more can be inserted with the system's own Character Palette, or by entering character values from the keyboard via the system's Unicode Hex Input keyboard layout. These features are accessed through a menu bar icon turned on in your System Preferences from the International panel. For details, see OS X's Help, or better yet, Matt Neuburg's excellent ebook *Take Control of What's New in Word 2004: Advanced Editing and Formatting.*

Among the useful symbols available for your documents are real marks for "copyright," "registered," and "trademark" to replace the typewriter equivalents created with parentheses. All these are on the Special Characters tab of the Symbols dialog box, where you can also find their keyboard shortcuts. Or Word can substitute the correct characters automatically, as set in the AutoCorrect dialog box on the "AutoFormat As You Type" tab.

(c)	©	(r)	®	(tm)	™
Wrong	Right	Wrong	Right	Wrong	Right

It's common to need occasional symbols from foreign languages. Today's Unicode fonts might handle symbols of many languages, while most fonts will at least handle symbols of European languages like French and German. If you don't want to use the Symbols Dialog box for the European languages, look in Word Help for keyboard shortcuts by searching on "international characters."

Also available in some fonts are the *prime* (Unicode 2032) and *double prime* (Unicode 2033). These are the correct symbols to use for inch and foot marks, or minute and second marks. As an alternative, though, you can use italicized straight quotes—and in fact, in some typefaces, you can't tell the difference. But never use curly quotes! If necessary, temporarily turn off the "smart quotes" option found on the "AutoFormat As You Type" tab.

ﾠ, ﾠ,,	ﾠʹ ﾠʺ	ﾠʹ ﾠʺ
Wrong	Maybe	Best

Fractions should always appear with a small raised numerator and with a small denominator. Also, it's best if they're divided by a true *fraction slash* or *bar* (Unicode 2044) instead of the more commonly seen *virgule,* or common slash.

1-1/2	1½	1½
Wrong	Maybe	Best

Later versions of Word can insert a few common fractions through AutoFormatting when you type the numbers separated by a common slash. Other fractions might be found within your font, while less common ones you'll have to build yourself. You may even find special superscript and subscript digits for this purpose in your Unicode font. If necessary, use kerning—explained in my chapter on perfecting your text—to bring the numbers closer to the slash. The fraction slash, however, generally includes built-in kerning.

Fonts commonly include math symbols like the plus sign (Unicode 002B), the minus sign (Unicode 2212), and the multiplication sign (Unicode 00D7), so you don't need to use substitutes.

X   ×

Maybe   Best

If there's a symbol that you use often but that doesn't have a keyboard shortcut, you can assign one of your own in the Symbol dialog box. Or just insert all the symbols you might need into a single document of their own, then copy and paste into your text as needed.

Note that, if the font you're using doesn't include the symbol you're trying to insert, later versions of Word may automatically use that symbol from a different font.

Also note that not all print services can handle all the newer symbols found in Unicode fonts, even if those symbols print properly on your desktop printer. For best results, use a print service with a digital press or other up-to-date equipment and avoid creating your PDF files with tools not normally used for professional output.*

---

* In the first proof for this book, fraction characters and the multiplication sign from Microsoft's Georgia font did not print properly from a file created with Mac OS X's built-in PDF features. In a second proof, made from a file generated by Acrobat for the Mac, those symbols printed correctly. (The problem symbols were "CID Type 2" characters—or "TrueType(CID)" characters—as found in Georgia in its Mac version only.)

Using Print Emphasis

Because a typewriter has only one font style—plain text— emphasis in text is most often shown by underlining. But underlining is almost never used in print, since there's no need for it. Bolding is sometimes used instead but can look brash and unprofessional. The traditional and best choice is italics.

<u>Middle</u> **Middle** *Middle*

Wrong   Maybe   Best

Word provides a number of ways to apply styles to fonts, but when typing text, the keyboard shortcuts are probably the most convenient. For italics, it's Control-I (Windows) or Command-I (Mac); for bold, Control-B (Windows) or Command-B (Mac). These are toggles, turning the styles either on or off. Just hit the shortcut once before typing the text you want emphasized, then again at the other end.

Don't forget to apply the style to any comma or period following the words!

For headings, just about any form of emphasis *except* underlining can be used to distinguish them from text and from each other. For instance, a chapter title might be in 18-point type and centered. A subhead for a topic might be in 14-point, all caps, flush left, in a different font. A *run-in heading*—one that starts a paragraph—might be in bold, italic, or bold italic. The important things are to make the formatting consistent, easy to recognize, and not overbearing.

Using Print Spaces

Don't put more than one space at the end of a sentence or after a colon, as you would on a typewriter. In print typography, spaces are always single, even if they vary in width. If you can't break the habit of typing two together, you can replace all pairs with single spaces by using the AutoFormat feature or the Replace command.

Sometimes, though, you may need a space wider than a normal one, or just a space that won't change width when Word justifies the line. Various possibilities are on the Special Characters tab of the Symbol dialog box. I've already mentioned the Nonbreaking Space. You could also choose an Em Space—a space as wide as the letter M in whatever font is in use—or an En Space—a space as wide as an N. In later versions of Word for Windows, you can also choose a ¼ Em Space.

If you need to spread text across the page, as for a table, never use spaces to position it. Use Word's Table feature instead. Or you can set margins and tabs, either on the ruler or in a format dialog box.

Using Print Paragraphs

In print, the *indented paragraph*—a paragraph with the first line indented from the others—is the kind normally used for most text. Never add this indent with spaces or a tab, as on a typewriter. Instead, set up the indent on the Ruler or in the Paragraph Format dialog box. Also, the half-inch indent customary on the typewriter is too large for most books. A better measurement might be ¼ or ⅜ inch.

Another kind of paragraph you'll need is the *block paragraph,* in which no lines are indented from one another.

In text with indented paragraphs, the block paragraph is normally used for the first paragraph of a chapter, or of a special section like the Introduction or Foreword, or of a block quote.

You might also use block paragraphs for speeches in a script, or if you want an "Internet look."

And sometimes you may need a *hanging paragraph,* in which the first line is *not* indented, but the rest are.
This might be used, for instance, in a bibliographic list of references, or in an index.
This indent too can be set on the Ruler or in the Paragraph Format dialog box.

Block paragraphs are the *only* ones that should be separated by space in between them. For the other paragraph types, the indent *takes the place* of space between. Never use both! When you're working with indents, make sure they're not carried over to any centered lines, as this will shift the line's content to the right.

Using Print Vertical Spacing

In most cases, avoid inserting blank lines to add empty space between text elements—paragraphs, headings, block quotes, or anything else. Instead, set Spacing Before and After in the Paragraph Format dialog box.

For instance, to separate block paragraphs, you would use Spacing After, preferably as part of a style. This gives you more control over height and makes later adjustments easier, and also keeps any of your pages from starting with a blank line.

To make sure that Spacing Before and After gives the results you expect, turn *on* the Compatibility option or preference "Don't use HTML paragraph auto spacing." This stops Word from overlapping adjacent spacing instead of adding it separately. Overlapping is standard in Web browsers, and for some odd reason, it has also been Word's default since Word 2000-2001. It can be very frustrating when you're trying to control spacing—especially if you don't know what Word is doing!

4
Formatting Your Text

As with most programs—from the lowliest word processor to the loftiest page layout program—getting fine type with Word is more a matter of knowing what you're doing than of Word's own capabilities. Here's much of what you'll need to know.

Choosing Your Fonts

Fonts—or more accurately, *typefaces*—can be classified in various ways. One of the most important divisions is between *proportional* and *monospace*. In proportional faces, letters and other characters vary in width. In monospace faces, the widths are all the same.

Middle   `Middle`

Proportional   Monospace

Why would you use a monospace typeface in your book? Unless you're aiming for a special effect, you wouldn't. Monospace faces are designed for typewriters, and are also commonly used in email to properly display spaced text. But for books, you need to know about these faces only so you can recognize and avoid using them!

Book typefaces come in two main varieties: *serif* and *sans serif*. A *serif* is a doohickey stuck at the end of the main strokes of a letter. *Sans serif* is simply French for "without serif." All this is just to say there are book faces with doohickeys, and book faces without.

Middle   Middle

Serif   Sans Serif

Serif typefaces are usually considered easier to read—though this may be just because we're more used to them. For this reason, we're generally advised to stick to serif faces for book text. Headings, on the other hand, can be serif or sans serif. It's common—though by no means necessary—to match a serif face in the text with a sans serif face for headings.

Besides serif and sans serif, there are a vast number of script and decorative typefaces. But their use in a book, if any, is generally only for titles.

One of the biggest mistakes made by beginners is to use too many typefaces, which makes a book look like a mess. So, stick to just one face for your book's text; and for the headings, add no more than one other.

Word's default typeface is Times New Roman—or the Mac's equivalent, Times—and many users never switch to another. But this narrow face, designed for newspaper columns, was never meant for books. Instead, set your body text in a serif face of more generous width—a face like Palatino, Garamond, Baskerville, Century Schoolbook, or Sabon.

Fonts—the files that supply the typefaces to your computer—come in various file formats, including PostScript, TrueType, OpenType, and more. PostScript fonts have a longer history in commercial printing, but print services that take PDF files should be able to handle any kind of high-quality font you embed, including the ones that came with your operating system or with Word. Beware, though, of cheapy fonts from unreliable sources, because they really can cause trouble. Also avoid the now little-used PostScript "Type 3" fonts, which are not recommended for commercial printing.

Also, make sure you have a separate font for each type style you intend to use with your typeface. For your book text, you should have separate fonts probably for both regular text and italic, and possibly for bold and bold italic as well. Unlike a page layout program, Word will obligingly fabricate a style for you on screen when the separate font is not on your computer. But even if you're using Acrobat for your PDF files, the style might look wrong in print or be omitted entirely, especially if the face is less common.

In Windows, you can check for these separate fonts in the Fonts control panel. In Mac OS X, open the Font Book application and click the triangle next to the typeface name.

If you're sending your book to your print service as a PDF file, make sure that each of your chosen fonts can be embedded in it. There won't be a problem with any font that comes with your computer operating system, Word, or most other programs. But if you have a font purchased separately, you need to check this, because some such fonts are restricted.

Frankly, the best way to avoid font problems of almost any kind is to stick to fonts that come with Word or Windows. These fonts have been tuned for Word, and Word knows just how to handle them to best effect. Fonts from another source may be superior—as are fonts from Adobe, for instance—but their advanced features are likely to be ignored by Word and may even cause it to choke.

In the past, for a book meant for print on demand, it was often considered wisest to stick to typefaces designed for the Web, like Microsoft's Georgia or Verdana. Such sturdier faces could look better than more delicate ones at the lower resolution of POD printing presses, especially at smaller font sizes. While these faces are still good choices, the resolution of POD presses used to print book pages has increased dramatically. It's now safe to use almost any book typeface inside—though for covers, it's still best to avoid delicate faces at small sizes.

All typefaces installed with current versions of Office or Word have been updated for Unicode printing, with useful characters never before easily available in Word. So, if you chose not to install these fonts before, you should probably go back and do it now. The encoding of old documents will be updated automatically to match the new font versions.

Choosing Your Font Size

Font size is measured in *points,* with 72 points to the inch. The measurement is taken from just above the highest part of the highest-reaching letter, to just below the lowest part of the lowest-reaching. By typing a value directly into Word's Font Size box, you can specify the size in increments of half a point.

Word's default font size is 10 points, but that's too small for almost any book other than a mass market paperback. For comfortable reading, larger font sizes should be used for longer lines of text. One rule of thumb says the optimum number of characters per line is around 40, and the maximum, around 70.

For the page sizes of typical trade books, you'll probably want to keep your body text type between 11 and 13 points. In part, the choice depends on the typeface, since some appear bigger or smaller than others at the same font size. Times New Roman and Times, for example, look much smaller than Georgia does.

Of course, there are advantages to using smaller font sizes in longer lines. This saves money by requiring fewer pages for the book, and also helps make your typesetting look more even. But if you overdo it, you risk being branded as amateur for producing text that's hard to read.

Choosing Your Vertical Spacing

Linespacing is the spacing between lines of text within a paragraph. Your needs may not be met by Word's standard choices—"single," "1.5," and "double." For more control, go to the Paragraph Format dialog box, then for "Line spacing" select "At least" or "Exactly" and enter a measurement. The "At least" setting will allow expansion for inline graphics. "Exactly" will prevent lines being forced apart by enlarged, raised, or lowered characters.

Like font size, linespacing is measured in *points,* at 72 to the inch, and Word allows control in half-point increments. For normal book text, a good measurement would be 2 to 4 points more than the font size—for instance, 14 to 16 points for 12-point type. The longer the line of text, the more linespacing needed to ease the reader from one line's ending to the start of the next—as well as to prevent the text from looking crowded.

Many designers like their text to line up exactly across facing pages—a nice touch, though not strictly necessary. To achieve this, the height of every element in the text block has to be specified as an exact multiple of the text linespacing. For instance, if your linespacing is 15 points and you set Spacing After for each paragraph, that setting too would be 15 points.

For other elements, you might have to do more arithmetic. For instance, though the space taken by a heading would have to be a multiple of 15 points, you could achieve this in various ways. One would be to give the heading an exact linespacing of 15, a Space Before of 18 points, and a Space After of 12 points. (Yes, it's OK to have an exact linespacing measurement smaller than the font size measurement, as long as there's Spacing Before.) But you could juggle those points between the three settings, as long as the total was divisible by 15.

Controlling Horizontal Spacing

Within text, there are two kinds of horizontal spacing. *Letterspacing*—sometimes called *tracking*—is the spacing between letters, while *wordspacing* is the spacing between words. As you might expect, increasing or decreasing letterspacing will also affect wordspacing—but not the other way around.

Though most page layout programs give you controls for both of these, Word allows adjustment of letterspacing only. Word calls this setting "Character Spacing," and it's on a tab of the Font Format dialog box. If you like, you can use this setting to give your text either a "looser" or a "tighter" look overall. For selected text or a style, choose "Expanded" or "Condensed" and enter a point size in increments of a tenth of a point. A little goes a long way!

Kerning is the moving of individual letters closer or farther apart to make the spacing *look* more even. For example, in the word *Word,* the *o* might be better moved slightly under the overhang of the *W.* (See the title page of this book.) Many fonts—especially the more professional ones—have built-in recommendations for automatic kerning of specific letter pairs.

Not all word processors pay attention to these kerning recommendations, but Word honors at least the most important ones if you want it to. This setting too is on the Character Spacing tab of the Font Format dialog box. You can apply it to selected text or to specific styles.

Generally, kerning should be applied to headings and any other type larger than normal text size. It may also be best to apply it to normal text, though this isn't considered necessary and may burden a slow computer. Unfortunately, Word for the Mac does *not* yet properly kern justified text, so Mac users should limit their kerning to headings. (That's what I've had to do in this book.)

In my chapter on perfecting your text, I'll discuss adjusting the kerning of individual letter pairs.

By the way, Microsoft's Georgia and Verdana typefaces are designed specifically to need little or no kerning. This makes them especially useful for any text that can't or won't be kerned.

Controlling Justification

Word offers all the usual options in alignment of text to the left and right margins—"Left," "Right," "Centered," or "Justified." These can be accessed in various ways, including in the Paragraph Format dialog box.

In books, text type is almost always *justified*—meaning that individual lines are stretched or squeezed to exactly fit between the left and right margins, so that text forms a straight edge at either side. There are various techniques a program can use to justify, and the more techniques a program combines, the better the result. Adobe InDesign, for example, has an option for stretching or squeezing space between letters as well as between words.

Word's default way of justifying is fairly limited. All it adjusts is the space between words—and even that is only stretched, not squeezed. Though this is usually adequate, it can leave lines looking a bit "loose" from excess space.

Luckily, there's an option buried deep in Word that lets you improve the way it justifies. Just go to your Compatibility Options or Preferences and select "Do full justification like WordPerfect 6.x for Windows." Now Word will be able to squeeze the space between words as well as stretch it.

If you're on a Mac, Word 2004 is the first version that makes this work properly—which is one reason I don't recommend earlier ones.

Controlling Hyphenation

To get justified lines with good spacing, you'll need to turn on Word's automatic hyphenation. To find this setting, choose "Hyphenation" from the Tools menu, or else "Language" and then "Hyphenation." (If the command is missing, then you somehow didn't install Word's Hyphenation tool.) While you're there, you can decide whether to turn on "Hyphenate words in CAPS." If this is off, Word won't try to hyphenate acronyms and such.

As with Word's default typeface and font size, its default hyphenation is better suited to newspaper columns than to books. For fewer and better hyphenated words, change the settings in the Hyphenation dialog box so that the hyphenation zone is increased to half an inch, and the limit on consecutive hyphens is reduced to two. The wider the hyphenation zone, the fewer the hyphens, but the more variation in wordspacing from one line to the next.

With hyphenation on for the document, you may need to restrict it for certain elements. Headings, for example, are never hyphenated. To turn it off, select the entire element—including the paragraph mark—then check "Don't hyphenate" on the Line and Page Breaks tab of the Paragraph Format dialog box. You can also add this setting to styles.

In my chapter on perfecting your text, I'll discuss adjusting the hyphenation of individual words.

Controlling Page Endings

It's important to make sure your pages don't start or end badly. The most common problems are *widows* and *orphans*. An *orphan* is a paragraph's first line that appears by itself at the bottom of a page, especially with a blank line or a heading above it. A *widow* is a paragraph's *last* line that appears by itself at the *top* of a page.

Word avoids most widows and orphans by default. To make sure this option is turned on, place your cursor in normal body text and check the Line and Page Breaks tab in the Paragraph Format menu. If the option is off, you can turn it on here after going back and selecting all text in the document. Better yet, add it to your body text styles.

Working with Word #4:
Using Styles

The Styles feature in Word is both a curse and blessing. It's a curse because setting up styles properly can be so difficult and tedious. It's a blessing because styles speed up the job of formatting and help make results more consistent. They also allow you to easily make formatting changes throughout your document and experiment with variations.

As I discuss in my chapter on formatting your text, Word requires numerous settings to achieve fine type. The most efficient way to deal with them is to include them in styles and apply them all together. In fact, the ideal would be to manage every element in the book with styles, using little or no direct formatting.

But what is a style? Basically, it's a collection of formatting settings that are applied all together to parts of your text. For instance, you could create a style called "Title Chapter" that specified a font, font size, and linespacing, made the text bold, centered it, added Spacing Before and After, told Word to keep the text on the same page as the following paragraph, and turned off hyphenation.

Later, if you changed some settings in the style, the change would be reflected automatically in all the text that the style governed. For instance, if you'd applied "Title Chapter" to all the chapter titles in your document, you could later change the font for all those titles at once by changing the font in the style.

In older versions of Word, you access style functions with the Style command on the Format menu. Later versions give you more convenient access in the Styles and Formatting task panel (Windows) or in the Styles pane of the Formatting Palette (Mac).

If you're using styles extensively, you might also want to try out Word's Style Area. This is an optional column to the left of your document in Normal View only, showing the name of the style used by each paragraph. You can even edit the style by double-clicking on its name. Activate the Style Area by setting a width for it in your View Options or Preferences.

Word offers several kinds of styles: character, paragraph, and in later versions, list and table. Of these, paragraph styles are the most important, covering nearly everything in your document. You can use Word's built-in styles as is—a terrible idea—or modify them, or create your own.

Besides format settings, each style is defined by certain basic properties that you can define freely. The first property of the style is what style it is based on. This is because most styles are created by adding format settings to another style.

For instance, if I have a document with several kinds of paragraph, I might start by creating a style called "Paragraph" with format settings that all those kinds would share. I'd then go on to create other styles based on "Paragraph." "Paragraph Indented" would add a first-line indent, "Paragraph Hanging" would indent every line except the first, and "Paragraph Block" would add space after the paragraph, with no indent.

After that, styles for even more specialized kinds of paragraph could be based on any of those three. In this way, my styles would become "hierarchical." And I could do something similar with all headings. The beauty of this approach is that I can change any number of styles by changing a style they're ultimately based on.

For instance, in the example above, if I changed the font in "Paragraph" from Times New Roman to Georgia, the same change would occur in every style based on "Paragraph," and in every style based on those, and so on—that is, as long as none of those other styles already had a differing font. But if in "Paragraph Block" I had already set the font to Verdana instead of Georgia, then Word would leave that alone. The font change in "Paragraph" would not affect either "Paragraph Block" or any style based on it.

Word itself uses a hierarchical scheme in the styles it supplies. All supplied styles are based ultimately on the one called "Normal." You can use the Normal style as your own ultimate base—either as is or with your own changes, as I've chosen to do myself. Some Word experts, though, prefer to create a base style from scratch, by basing a style on "no style."

The second option for a style is what style will be applied when you start the following paragraph. This is a simple device for automatically assigning a style so you don't have to do it by hand. For instance, if you were typing a paragraph in your style "Paragraph Indented" and you started a new paragraph, chances are you would want it to be in the same style. On the other hand, you probably wouldn't want two paragraphs in a row to have the style "Title Chapter."

In Word, any format setting you can apply directly to text can also be applied to a style. In later versions, basic format settings are included on the main panel of the Style dialog box—but to access *all* options in any version, use the pull-down Format menu at the bottom of the panel.

When creating or editing a style, the dialog box gives you the choice of saving the style to the template your document is based on. This is good if you want that certain style with those certain properties to be available to all other documents based on that template.

You can also choose to "Automatically update" the style. This means that, if you later change the style in the template directly or from a different document, the modified style will be applied to the current document the next time you open it. I advise against this, because it allows Word to modify your document's formatting in a way you may not intend, and even without your realizing it. You can always update your document's styles manually with the Style Gallery, or by copying them to your document with the Organizer.

If you copy and paste text of a certain style from another document, that text will be reformatted if the new document includes a style with the same name but different properties. But if there's no style of that name in the new document, the style of that text will be added. Be careful not to copy and paste the other document's final paragraph mark, or you might entirely replace some of the new document's styles!

5
Perfecting Your Text

When it comes to formatting, Word, like almost any other word processor or page layout program, can do only so much on the basis of general settings. At some point, you have to step in and make adjustments.

Fixing Letterspacing

Word's automatic kerning takes care of most needed adjustment of spacing between letters. In some cases, though, you may wish to give it some help by kerning manually. This is especially true for elements on your title page or book cover, where the type is big enough to make any problems more evident.

To manually kern a pair of letters, select just the first of the letters. On the Character Spacing tab of the Font Format dialog box, set Spacing to "Expanded" or "Condensed" and specify the amount. Or select just the last letter of a word to expand or condense the space between that word and the next.

Fixing Line Endings

Sometimes at the end of a line, Word breaks a word or phrase where you don't want it to—or fails to break one where you do want. You have a number of tools at hand for dealing with these situations. (To see what you're doing, make sure Word is set to show formatting marks.)

Word's hyphenation is impressively accurate, but if you do see a break you don't like, you can always place your cursor at your preferred break point and insert an Optional Hyphen. You can enter this from the Special Characters tab of the Symbol dialog box, or from the keyboard with Control-Hyphen (Windows) or Command-Hyphen (Mac).

If you don't want the word hyphenated at all, you have a couple of options. The simplest is to end the line early with a Manual Line Break—Shift-Return or Shift-Enter on your keyboard. The problem with this, of course, is that you'll probably need to remove the break if you later add or remove text above it in the paragraph. (If your Manual Line Break causes the line to stop short of the right margin, go to your Compatibility Options or Preferences and turn *off* "Don't expand character spaces on the line ending Shift-Return.")

You can also turn off hyphenation for just that word. Select the word, then go to the Language dialog box and set the language to "no proofing," or check the option "Do not check spelling or grammar." Just make sure beforehand that the word is spelled correctly! You can also add these settings to styles.

Sometimes the spot where you don't want the line to end is at a hyphen or a space. Two tools for controlling this are the Nonbreaking Space and the Nonbreaking Hyphen. Instead of telling Word where you want the break, these tell Word where you don't.

For instance, if you had "J. R. R. Tolkien" in your text, you would want spaces between the initials, but you'd want Word to keep all the initials on one line. To guarantee this, you'd use the Nonbreaking Space between them. This can be inserted from the Special Characters tab of the Symbol dialog box, or from the keyboard with Control-Shift-Space (Windows) or Option-Space (Mac).

Similarly, if you wanted to keep "A-1" on one line, you would use a Nonbreaking Hyphen. This symbol too can be inserted from the Special Characters tab, or with Control-Shift-Hyphen (Windows) or Command-Shift-Hyphen (Mac).

In some cases, you might want Word to optionally break a string of characters *without* showing a hyphen—for instance, after a slash in a Web address such as "www.aaronshep.com/ publishing." In later versions of Word for Windows, you can do this by entering a No-Width Optional Break from the Special Characters tab. Or in later versions for either Windows or Mac, enter a Zero Width Space (Unicode 200B). If that's too complicated, or for earlier Word versions, you can jury rig by adding a space with a font size of 1 point.

By the way, in later versions of Word for Windows, the Special Characters tab also offers a No-Width Non Break. You might think this could be used to stop hyphenation between two letters, but in fact it seems to be useful only for some languages other than English.

Fixing Paragraphs

At this writing, both Quark and PageMaker justify text basically the same way Word does—one line at a time. InDesign's big claim to fame is that it justifies text a *paragraph* at a time, looking back at previous lines in the paragraph for solutions to any spacing problems that come up.

The big secret, though, is that you can do that manually yourself, even with a word processor. Your tools for this are the Manual Line Break and the Optional Hyphen, which I've already described.

Say you find a line with words spread too far apart. Look closer to the beginning of that paragraph for lines that have wordspacing *tighter* than average and that end with a short word or with a single syllable of a hyphenated word. If you find one, try inserting a Manual Line Break to shift the final letters to the next line. With luck, this will shuffle the paragraph in a way that gets rid of your problem without creating a new one.

An Optional Hyphen too can sometimes be used to shift final letters to the next line, or to move letters up from the line below. This overrides your hyphenation settings, as you may need to do now and then, especially with the conservative settings I recommended.

Other instances in which you might want to make such adjustments include:

- If a paragraph is hyphenated too often or unattractively.
- If a word is hyphenated between pages or columns.
- If a paragraph's last line looks stubby because it's a single small word or a partial word, or shorter than the next paragraph's indent.
- If spaces between words line up vertically to create a "river" in the text.

• If identical words or phrases line up vertically.

• If a line's wordspacing is too tight (as can happen with "WordPerfect justification" turned on as I recommend).

When the usual tools don't help to fix a paragraph's line endings, you can also try stretching or squeezing the space between all its characters at once. As I mentioned before, this can be done on the Character Spacing tab of the Font Format dialog box. Be sure to first select the *entire paragraph*. To avoid being obvious, you probably don't want a change of more than a tenth of a point either way.

If you're *really* desperate, you can edit the paragraph to add or subtract text. But I don't recommend this unless you're the author!

Of course, before starting manual adjustment of any kind, make sure your text is as close to final form as possible. Otherwise, your adjustments will be one more thing to redo when the text is revised.

If you do need to start over, Word's Find and Replace can quickly remove Manual Line Breaks. Use the Special pull-down menu for the Find field and leave the Replace field empty. Be careful not to remove any Manual Line Breaks you've entered for other purposes.

Does Word require a lot of manual adjustment, then? Not really. As a rough guideline, one paragraph out of ten might call for work, and much of that would be optional. Once you get the hang of it, adjusting a book such as the one you're reading might take less than an hour.

Fixing Page Endings

Just as Word has tools for fixing individual line endings, so it has tools for individual page endings. Of course, you can always force a page to end with a Manual Page Break. But more flexible tools are located on the Line and Page Breaks tab of the Paragraph Format dialog box. Any of these settings can be applied to selected text or added to styles.

The "Keep lines together" setting guarantees that an entire paragraph will appear on the same page. This might help, for example, if you don't want to end a page in the middle of one verse of a poem, or one speech in a play.

"Keep with next" will stop a paragraph from appearing at a page bottom without the following paragraph. Probably the most important use for this is to prevent a subheading from appearing without any text below it. The setting could also be used to glue captions to graphics, or questions to answers.

"Page break before" is equivalent to placing a Manual Page Break before a paragraph. You could use this, for instance, to set a subheading style so that each subheading would start a new page.

Ideally, each facing pair of full text pages would have the same number of lines, which would perfectly line up across the spread. But what with avoiding widows and orphans and with other special adjustments, it's not likely that all your facing text pages will match. Then how do you correct for this?

There are several schools of thought. One recommends *vertical justification,* in which linespacing is expanded when necessary to produce a text block of standard height, even if it ruins the alignment of individual lines across the facing pages.

Word does offer a "Justified" setting for Vertical Alignment, found on the Layout tab of the Page Setup dialog box

(Windows) or the Document Format dialog box (Mac). But it's designed only for special cases like title pages. Used on normal text, it leaves linespacing as is and only expands space between paragraphs—and it insists on vertically justifying the last page of a section even if that page isn't nearly full. So vertically justifying a full document really isn't an option with Word.

A second school recommends evening up the page bottoms even if it means making some page pairs shorter. This involves going through the document from front to back and wherever necessary adding Manual Page Breaks to force a line or two from the bottom of one page to the top of the next. (Though some specialized typesetting programs can perform this job automatically, the high-end page layout programs can't do that any more than Word can.)

In some cases, to make your pages come out right, you might have to resort to your paragraph-smoothing tricks to add or subtract text lines. But however you do it, it's a tedious job, and if you later edit your text, you have to do it over.

Then there's the third school, which I belong to. This one says it's not worth the trouble, and advises you to leave your page bottoms uneven.

It's up to you.

6
Handling Special Text

A book contains a number of text elements other than the main text and headings. Here's how to deal with some of them.

Handling Lists

Ironically, two of Word's simplest functions for special text are ones that don't work well and that you should probably avoid: bulleting and list numbering. Word has been prone to corrupting documents that use these, especially if applied apart from a style.

Another good reason to manually add all bullets and list numbers is that the fonts of the ones added automatically by Word may not embed properly in PDF files. You can add bullets manually from the Symbol dialog box, or with Option-8 on the Mac. For tidy alignment of the text that follows, place tab characters after the bullets or numbers—not regular spaces, since their widths will vary with line justification.

If automatic bulleting or numbering has already been applied, you can remove it by selecting the paragraphs and clicking the Bullets or Numbering button in the toolbar to turn it off. Or you can use the Bullets and Numbering command on the Format menu and select "None" for each feature. Or if it's part of a style, just change or clear the style.

Handling Headers and Footers

To edit a section's headers and footers in Print or Page Layout View, just double-click on an existing header or footer area; or in either that view or Normal View, place your cursor in the section, then choose "Header and Footer" from the View menu. (In Normal View, that will switch Word to Print or Page Layout View.) A Header and Footer toolbar will appear, and you can use its buttons to navigate among all your headers and footers.

By default, each type of header or footer in a section is identical to and linked to the same type of header or footer in the section before. For instance, if you've placed each chapter in its own section, and the even header of chapter 1 says "American Pie," then the even header of your chapter 2 will also say "American Pie" unless you change it. You would see this status in the Header and Footer toolbar by looking at the "Same as Previous" button, which would appear depressed as long as the two headers were linked.

To change this header in chapter 2, you would first have to click the "Same as Previous" button to release it. This is important! If you edited the header *before* unlinking it, you would also be editing the even header in chapter 1, as well as the even headers in any previous sections it linked to! But after the chapter 2 header was unlinked, you could safely make any changes you liked. Of course, these changes would show up also in any later sections that had their even headers still linked to that one!

Because of the need to link or unlink headers and footers, you can sometimes run into a problem where you want to edit a header or footer that is not visible in Print or Page Layout View. For instance, if your title page is in a section of its own and that section is set to have a different first page, you can access only the first-page header and footer, not the ones for even or odd pages.

There are a several solutions to this. One is to go to the following section and edit the corresponding header or footer while it's set for "Same as Previous." Another is to temporarily insert page breaks within the short section, creating extra pages to display the other headers and footers.

In Word 2004 for the Mac, you can also try the Header and Footer pane, a separate pane that appears in Normal View when needed, much like the Footnotes pane. You can turn it on in your View Preferences. This is a reappearance of a long discontinued feature that was actually a more efficient way of editing book headers and footers. Unfortunately, editing in this pane in Word 2004 can produce strange behavior—so proceed with caution if you try it.

As wonderfully convenient as is Word's automatic place-ment of headers and footers, setting them up properly in the first place can be confusing and frustrating. This is partly because, like other section properties, headers and footers are stored in the section break at the *end* of the section—or for the last section, in the final paragraph mark.

To make things easy on yourself, insert all of a book's sec-tion breaks *before* creating headers and footers. Then work from beginning to end, defining headers and footers for each section in turn, and remembering to unlink any header or footer before changing it. If you do get hopelessly muddled, the best thing might be to replace all section breaks with page breaks—you can use Word's Find and Replace to do it all at once—and just start over.

Handling Page Numbering

Of course, Word also handles page numbering automatically. In your header or footer, just put your cursor where you want the number to appear, then click the "Insert Page Number" button on the toolbar. For each section, you can also tell Word what number to start on, and what number format to use. To do this, choose "Page Numbers" from the Insert menu, then click on "Format."

In the past, this capability might have been used to number a book's beginning pages in Roman numerals, then start over with conventional ones. That practice is now outdated, but there are a number of other possible uses.

For instance, I always number the pages of my books from the title page, but I often add two or more pages before that for promotional copy. To do this, I set up the initial pages to have odd and even headers and footers—just like the rest of the book—but I leave them blank, with no page numbers or anything else. Then I put my cursor on the title page, which starts a new section, and I restart the numbering—though of course, that page is set up as a "Different first page," with its header and footer blank.

Just remember: The odd page numbers always go on the right!

Handling Footnotes and Endnotes

Word is well known for its competent handling of footnotes and endnotes—something that can be quite a problem even in some top page layout programs. In Word, the notes automatically appear in the correct position and follow text if it shifts to a different page or chapter.

Both footnotes and endnotes are inserted with the Footnote command on the Insert menu. This brings up a dialog box, and if you click the Options button, you'll get a number of formatting choices for all your notes together. For instance, if you've placed section breaks between chapters, you can choose to restart footnote numbering with each chapter, or to place endnotes at the end of each chapter rather than at the end of the book.

You can also choose the number format and whether to place a footnote always at the bottom of the page or instead directly under the text.*

You can edit footnotes and endnotes directly in Print or Page Layout View. In Normal View, the Footnotes command on the View menu brings up a separate editing pane with all your notes together.

---

* I like to keep my footnotes at the bottom of the page.

Handling Automated Text

As you might expect from one of the world's premier document processors, Word can automatically compile a variety of book elements. These include tables of contents, indexes, caption numbers, and cross-references. To accomplish much of this, Word sometimes uses text identified by certain styles, sometimes hidden text, and sometimes data placed in special *fields*.

Tables of contents can be generated automatically from headings, with a number of levels. Word provides a variety of formats, and you can also create your own. Indexes can be compiled from topics you flag in the text, or from terms you tell Word to flag for you.

For some of these automatic functions, you're required to insert "fields" into your text for Word to process, while for others, Word inserts a field to show the results. In your View Options or Preferences, you can change how fields show up on screen. For instance, while you're working with them, you might want to tell Word to show "Field codes." Otherwise, Word just shows a result—which is of course what you normally want.

You can also ask Word to always shade the fields, so that you can tell that a field result isn't editable text. This shading shows up only on screen, not in printing or in a PDF file.

In your Print Options or Preferences, you can set Word to "Update fields" before printing. This will update all page numbers in your automatic table of contents, index, and cross-references. To update without printing, just go into Print Preview.

If you're creating a table of contents in Word for Windows, make sure the dialog box option "Use hyperlinks instead of page numbers" is off. Though this option applies mostly to Web pages, it affects print documents too.

Personally, I don't use most of Word's automatic functions. If you're not revising a document frequently, changing these references yourself can be simpler than setting them up to be done just as you want. But the functions are there if you need them.

Handling Indexes

Though I don't bother with most of Word's automatic functions for special text, the exception is indexing. Word excels at this one, letting you choose between detailed control and the convenience of Word's own assistance.

Word offers two basic methods of preparing an index. The first requires manually marking up your text. You go through and insert hidden code to show what pages should be listed under what terms. Then Word looks at what you've done and automatically generates the index with page numbers, letting you format it as you like. If you're good at indexing, this is the method that produces the most comprehensive, sophisticated, and accurate results.

The second method is to let Word mark up the text for you. You must still tell Word what terms to look for and what terms to index under, but Word inserts all the hidden code itself. Then, as in the first method, it uses the code to generate the index. This is the method used for this book.

There are definite disadvantages to automatic markup. You're limited to indexing things that can be easily located with single words or short phrases. Broad concepts may not be easily identifiable. For instance, you might have a series of stories about "xenophobia"—but if you don't use the word "xenophobia" or an equivalent on each page of those stories, Word won't be able to properly index for that term.

From the other side, you may pick up references you don't want. If your book talks about "dogs" in some places and "hot dogs" in others, then your index entry for "dogs" will include references to both canines and food. (In fact, I had that problem with a pair of terms in this book—but I can't mention them on this page, or Word will index them again!)

Automatic markup also means no indexing levels, no cross-referencing, and no page ranges, either. Pages are always listed individually.

Then why would you use automatic markup? One simple reason is speed. Compiling and refining the terms you give Word can take time—almost three days for this book!—but manual markup could double the time it would take you to complete all steps.

The greater reason, though, is flexibility, especially if you expect to revise or update your book after publication. The first versions of this book included no index, because I felt that the complications of adjusting manual markup would discourage me from updating the book. But when I tried out automatic markup for another book, I realized I could do the bulk of the work for this one just once and then quickly apply it to all later versions.

Automatic markup, then, can be a very practical compromise between having a first-class index and having none at all. And an index produced this way can certainly be useful, if prepared properly.

For automatic markup, you provide your indexing terms to Word by creating a *concordance*. Start with a new, blank document, named anything you like. Now, at the very start of the document, insert a table with two columns. Everything else about the table can be left to Word's defaults. This table for your terms is the *only* thing you'll put in this file.

Next, find a word or phrase in your text that you want Word to index. Type, paste, or drag this into the table, in a cell in the left-hand column. In the right-hand cell of the same row, put the term you want Word to index it *under*. For instance, if the term in your text is "box," you might want to index it under "boxes."

This tells Word to index "box" under "boxes" *every* time the term shows up in the text. But of course, you also want Word to index every *variation* of "box." Unfortunately, Word isn't smart enough to work out such things for itself, so you have to add all likely variations to the concordance.

For instance, along with the singular "box," you'd probably want to list at least

- The plural "boxes."
- The capitalized plural "Boxes," in case it shows up at the beginning of a sentence. To Word, the capital letter makes it a different term! (A sentence isn't likely to begin with a capitalized singular, but you'd add that too if the term will appear in a heading.)
- The possessive "box's." Note that Word, at least in current versions, will *not* index single-word possessives. But this bug is acknowledged by Microsoft, so we can hope it will at some point be fixed. Meanwhile, in the hope of that day, it's probably best to include the possessives in your concordance.

Word ignores character formatting like italics when finding terms in the text, so you don't have to include that kind of variation.

But then there are the *types* of boxes you'd want indexed under the same term. So, for instance, you might also need to include "carton," "cartons," "Cartons," and "carton's."

Each of these variations on "box" or "carton" would go in the left-hand cell of a new row, and on each of those rows, "boxes" would go in the right-hand cell.

But wait! Don't you want "carton," etc., to be indexed also under "cartons"? Well, of course you do! So, you repeat those variations in a new set of rows, but this time putting "cartons" in each right-hand cell.

The whole thing would now look like this:

box	boxes
boxes	boxes
Boxes	boxes
box's	boxes
carton	boxes
cartons	boxes
Cartons	boxes
carton's	boxes
carton	cartons
cartons	cartons
Cartons	cartons
carton's	cartons

Oops! We forgot to include the general case that boxes fit under: "container," "containers," "Containers," "container's." . . . But you get the idea.

Keep going through the text till you've identified everything your readers are likely to want to look up. You can add rows as you go along just by pressing the Tab key from the last table cell. To add a row in the middle of the table, use the "Insert" command on the Table menu. To help you see what you've done, you can occasionally sort the table on either column with the "Sort" command on the Table menu. (Word itself, though, does not require that the terms be in any order.)

The term in the right-hand column should be entered exactly as you want it to appear in the index. For instance, if it's a book title, you'll want to italicize it.

But note that there are some kinds of entries that Word simply won't index under. These include terms enclosed by double quotes, and terms with single-character fractions. (That's why the index for this book doesn't include the full wording of any options or preferences, or any entry for the ¼ Em Space.)

As you can imagine from the example above, a concordance can grow quite long. The one for this book—double the size of any other I've done—is 23 pages. That's letter-size pages!

Word for Windows can edit tables of that length with no problem, but Word 2004 for the Mac starts choking on tables only half as long. One workaround is to split the concordance into multiple files and tell Word to mark up the text with one at a time. Or build your concordance as a simple list, inserting a tab between left-hand and right-hand terms, then use Word's "Convert Text to Table" command when you're ready to index. Or if you have a copy of Word for Windows, you could create your concordance in that, instead.

Of course, with automatic markup, your final index can be no better than the concordance you create. So, take some time to make it as comprehensive and useful as possible.

When a document is marked up for indexing, this adds a lot of gunk in the form of hidden code. Word offers no way to remove it in one shot—you have to go through and delete each entry by hand. There's also no way to automatically update the code when the document is revised. Repeating the automatic markup just adds a second set of entries.

For these reasons, I recommend that you *never* mark up your original document. Instead, each time you want to generate the index, make a copy of the document and produce the index from that. With automatic markup, there's little penalty for always starting fresh.

The one tricky thing about preparing your document for automatic markup is that you want Word to skip indexing most of your front matter—such as the title page and the table of contents—and maybe some or all of your back matter—such as the bibliography. If the parts to be skipped fall at the end of the book, you can simply delete them from your indexing copy—

but for anywhere else in the book, you have to make sure you don't change other page numbering.

There are two ways to do that. The first is to compensate for deletions by adding Manual Page Breaks. For instance, say you have a three-page table of contents, with section breaks before and after to start new pages. You would delete the complete text of the table of contents and replace it with two page breaks, giving you three blank pages.

The other way is to adjust the starting page number. For instance, let's say that you want to start indexing on page 9. You could delete everything up to that page, then use the Page Number Format dialog box to number the first page as 9. (To find that dialog box, use the "Page Numbers" command on the Insert menu, then click the "Format" button.)

Whichever way you choose, check the page number of the final page to be indexed, both before and after you make your adjustments, to make sure the numbering hasn't changed. Your index won't be much good if everything is off by a page or two!

At this point, your grunt work is mostly done, and it's time to let Word take over. Call up the Index and Tables dialog box with either the "Reference" or "Index and Tables" command on the Insert menu. (It doesn't matter at this point where your cursor is.)

On the Index tab, click on AutoMark, then locate your concordance file for Word. In about as long as it's taking me to type this sentence, Word will have marked up the entire document using the terms in your concordance.

Chances are, you'll now be looking at all the bits of ugly code that Word has added. If so, make them invisible with the "Show/Hide" toolbar button, or by changing your View Options or Preferences so that hidden text is not displayed. *This is important.* If the code is visible, it changes the paging of your document, and the whole index will be off!

All right, it's time for the final payoff. Place your cursor on a new, blank page at the end of your marked document. Return to the Index and Tables dialog box, choose your formatting options, and click "OK." In a ridiculously short time—just a few seconds—you'll see your complete index appear. It really is quite impressive.

Word deposits its results in the form of a single, uneditable field. To allow formatting and editing, convert it to regular text. Just click anywhere in the index to select the entire field, then press Control-Shift-F9 (Windows) or Command-Shift-F9 (Mac). You can now copy and paste the index into your original document and format and edit it as you like. (Just make sure you place it *after* all your indexed pages!)

Of course, you'll want to carefully look over the index to make sure that Word did what you expected and that you're happy with the results. Be sure to check a few of the index's page numbers against your document too, to make sure nothing went off.

If you see problems or ways to improve the results—which is likely, the first time or two for a book—just go back to your concordance and make the needed changes. If you left the indexing copy of your document open, you can remove the markup and start fresh just by clicking the "Undo" toolbar button a few times. If you didn't, it takes only a few minutes to prepare a new document copy for markup.

Look at other indexes to choose a suitable format. The index in this book uses a typical one, with double columns, a smaller font size, and hanging indents.

7
Handling Graphics

Though Word was not originally designed to handle much in the way of graphics, its abilities have gradually evolved. Here's what you can expect at present.

Preparing Graphics

Word handles two basic kinds of graphics. The first kind is *bitmap graphics,* or what Word loosely calls *pictures.* This is the kind handled by "photo-paint programs" like Adobe Photoshop. It includes photos from your camera, and art from your scanner. Though Word includes tools for editing pictures, you'll usually get better results if you work with a photo-paint program and then place the result in Word.

The second kind of graphics is *vector graphics,* or what Word calls *drawing objects.* This is the kind handled by "draw programs" like Adobe Illustrator. With this kind, the situation is the opposite: Graphics taken from most draw programs are unlikely to work properly—especially in Word for Windows. You're better off producing them from scratch in Word or taking them from other Microsoft programs.

In later versions of Word for Windows, Word displays a "drawing canvas" for you when you start to draw. This can be helpful if you're creating a complex graphic. But if you just want to draw a simple shape directly into the document, you can get rid of the canvas by pressing either Control-Z, Backspace, Esc, or Del before continuing. Or turn the feature off completely in your General Options.

Bitmap graphics and vector graphics are both defined in part by their *color mode.* Word can handle graphics in black and white, "grayscale," or RGB—the native full-color mode of computer monitors, scanners, and digital cameras.

With these color modes, Word works just fine for commercial black-and-white printing. Your print service will automatically convert grayscale and even RGB graphics to black and white by color reduction and *screening*—conversion from "continuous" tones to a pattern of tiny black dots.

But don't think that Word's RGB capability suits it to work on color publications. Full-color printing presses require a different color mode, CMYK. Today, digital presses *can* automatically convert RGB graphics to CMYK, and some may even do a good job of it—and in fact, you can convert them yourself when creating your PDF file with a program like Acrobat. But your ability to control the color tones in these cases is limited, and another issue—ironically related not to graphics but to type—will normally mean a serious compromise in quality.

I discuss this more in my chapter on producing a cover and even offer a possible workaround. Still, if you're producing a full-color book, I recommend that you forget Word and use a professional page layout program instead.

To keep file sizes down, use the "lowest" color mode appropriate to your graphic. In other words, if you use a "black-and-white" photo, you'll usually want it in grayscale, not RGB. If it's a scan of an ink drawing, you'll usually want it in black and white only.

Bitmap graphics are also defined by their *resolution,* normally measured in pixels per inch (ppi). For pictures that you send for commercial printing, the standard resolution is 300 ppi. That's for continuous-tone pictures like photos and paintings. If the picture is "line art"—such as an ink or pencil sketch—or if it includes small text, you'll want at least 600 ppi, and ideally 1200, for cleaner, smoother lines. Generally, don't use a higher resolution than you need, because that will greatly increase file size and burden Word.

Though Word will import a wide variety of graphics formats, you'll generally do best to avoid Web formats like JPEG and GIF. These formats compromise image quality to reduce file size. If you're taking digital photos for publication and must use JPEG, make sure the camera is set for least compression and highest image quality.

Generally, the best format for pictures you mean to insert into Word is TIFF, which any photo-paint program can save in. Be sure to flatten any layers before final saving. Also, to reduce file sizes, take advantage of any available "lossless" type of compression, such as LZW or Zip. Unlike JPEG—a compression method as well as a graphics format—lossless compression won't hurt your pictures.

Pictures print best when they offer a wide variety of tones, from pure black to pure white, with most of the picture in the middle range. To produce such a picture, get to know your photo-paint program's *histogram* and *levels controls*. Also get handy with its *unsharp mask* for sharpening photos and scans.

If your photo-paint program allows you to pre-screen your grayscale graphics or specify a screen resolution—don't. Leave all that to your print service. In fact, if you're starting with screened photos from a previous publication, be sure to de-screen them with your scanning or photo-paint program.

Print on demand is generally limited to extremely low-resolution screens—about the same as used by newspapers. For that and other reasons, quality of POD graphics has been a great source of complaint. But new presses and new technology are now improving things quite a bit. It's unclear whether POD graphics will approach offset quality any time soon, but at least they're no longer likely to look grossly unprofessional.

Still, graphics are not yet POD's strong point, and you may want to design around this weakness. Photos come out least well, cartoon-like pictures don't do badly, and simple line art does best of all. Keeping your graphics large can also help, as less detail will be lost.

If graphics are important to your book, be sure it's printed on pure white paper instead of the more common cream, or "natural." With a POD printing service, this may require you to produce your book at a different trim size, though the range of choices has been improving.

For more on preparing graphics, I recommend *The Official Adobe Print Publishing Guide,* by Brian P. Lawler, and *Better Gray in Print on Demand,* by Martin Koch.

Placing Graphics

There are two basic ways to place your prepared graphic in a Word document. The best way in most cases is to *insert* it. Put your cursor where you want the graphic, then select "Picture" from the Insert menu, then "From File."

You'll be given several options. You can simply add the graphic to your document and save it in your Word file. This is best if you have only small graphics or just a few. Or instead of storing it in your document, you can just link to the original graphic file, telling Word where to grab it when you print or create a PDF file. This is useful if you have a large number of high-resolution graphics, because it will stop your Word file from growing too large. You'll still see a low-resolution preview in Word. With this choice, you'll need to keep the graphic file in a stable location on your computer so that Word can find it.

You can also save the graphic in your Word file *and* link to the original file. This way, if you edit the graphic in the original file, the graphic in your document is updated automatically the next time your Word file is opened.

The other way to place the graphic is to paste it. This gives you an alternative if inserting gives you odd results or fails entirely. Open the graphic in your graphics program, select all of it, copy it, then paste it into Word. In Word for Windows, it's best to do this with the Paste Special command, which gives you several destination formats as options. "Bitmap" is probably the safest and most reliable.

The main downside to pasting a graphic instead of inserting and saving in the file is that Word won't compress the graphic, so your file size will be greater. But for a book with a small number of black-and-white or grayscale pictures, the difference probably won't be enough to matter.

In Word 2004 for the Mac, pasting is generally the *only* way you should place a pure black-and-white picture. If you insert it instead, Word will convert it to grayscale and antialias it—smooth all lines and edges but make them fuzzy—while also downsampling if the resolution is over 300 ppi. (The other way around all this is to first use a graphics program to convert the picture to EPS format, which Word 2004 will leave alone. This even lets you import a CMYK graphic!)

To find all options and settings for a graphic in your document, double-click it to bring up its dialog box. Or select the graphic, then look on the Format menu, where a new item will have appeared. Check in this dialog box to see whether Word reduced the size of your graphic, which it will do if an inserted picture was too large to fit within your margins. On the other hand, if you pasted a picture in Word for Windows, you'll have to reduce the size yourself to squeeze it back down to its original dimensions and resolution.

In the format dialog box, you'll be able to choose between two basic kinds of positioning for your graphic. The default is to leave the graphic in line with the text, so that the graphic moves with it both horizontally and vertically. Not all page layout programs let you do this, so it's an advantage of Word! Keep in mind that you may have to adjust the paragraph's linespacing to allow all of the graphic to show.

The second choice is to make the graphic "float" on the page, tethered to the text but not part of it. You do this by choosing any of the offered "Wrapping styles" other than "In line with text." You can place your graphic in front of the text or behind it, or make text flow around it in various ways. Note that you must be in Print or Page Layout View or in Print Preview to see floating graphics.

Floating your graphic allows several advanced options. You can choose among various automatic alignments to the page or to elements within it; you can specify an absolute position within one hundredth of an inch; or you can choose a "Book layout" alignment that flips the position for odd and even pages. By choosing "Move object with text," you can make the graphic follow the text vertically even without moving horizontally.

Word's floating is closer to how a page layout program works, but this feature is more limited. Even if a floating graphic doesn't follow text, it's still "anchored" to a specific paragraph on the same page. To see the anchor—and it actually looks like an anchor on screen—you have to be in Print or Page Layout View and select the graphic. You also have to have "Object anchors" turned on in your View Options or Preferences, or else "Show All." The anchor is shown at the start of the paragraph, but it's actually stored in the paragraph mark at the end.

This anchoring may affect your work in several ways. One is that, if you delete the paragraph mark that holds the anchor, the graphic goes with it! Also, if an anchoring paragraph shifts to a different page, so does the graphic, though usually taking an identical position on the new page. Finally, when you move a graphic, its anchor normally moves too, attaching itself to the closest paragraph.

It's easy to change which paragraph a graphic is anchored to. Just click on the anchor and drag it to whatever paragraph you like, on whatever page you like. In the format dialog box, you can also "Lock anchor" to keep the anchor attached to that paragraph no matter where on the page you move the graphic.

What you *can't* do is lock the anchor to a paragraph on one page while moving the graphic to another. The graphic must always be on the same page as its anchor. Among other things, this means it's impossible to insert a page-size illustration and get regular text to flow from the page before to the page after. For that kind of layout, you really do need a page layout program.

If you have a complex layout with overlapping graphics, you can use the Arrange or Order command from the Draw menu on the Drawing toolbar to move selected graphics forward or backward in relation to others. You can also use the command to move graphics behind or in front of text.

To make a graphic repeat from page to page, just insert it while editing your headers and footers. If the graphic is floating, it can appear anywhere on the page, not just in the header or footer area.

Large graphics can slow down the display of Word documents. If this becomes a problem, go to your View Options or Preferences and select "Picture placeholders" or "Image placeholders." You'll then see a box in place of each inline graphic, while the graphics still print as before. (Floating graphics aren't affected.) Note that in some Word versions this option or preference applies only to the current document.

8
Enhancing Your Layout

Though Word will never equal a top page layout program in handling complex layouts, it certainly provides the means to add variety and special touches to your pages.

Adding Tables

Word's Tables feature is excellent for creating—well, for creating tables! But besides its obvious use, it's handy for sticking together small, related graphic and text elements and positioning them as a unit.

What you *don't* want to use a Word table for is as a container for large amounts of text. This makes exact text positioning and alignment very difficult.

You can insert a table from the Table menu or with the "Insert Table" button on the toolbar. Keep in mind that tables extending from one page to the next can slow Word down. You'll also want to avoid *nested tables*—tables placed one in another.

Adding Text Boxes and Frames

Unlike a page layout program, Word doesn't use text boxes as primary text containers. Still, it does let you create them for special purposes.

To draw one, just choose "Text Box" from the Insert menu, click on your page, and drag. (In Word for Windows, if a large box appears saying, "Create your drawing here," press the Esc key, then turn off the General option "Automatically create drawing canvas when inserting AutoShapes.") Add your text to the box and push it around just as in a page layout program. You can even include graphics along with text.

To format the box, double-click its border, and a dialog box will appear. You can also select the box and choose "Text Box" from the Format menu. (The menu item appears only when the box is selected.) From there, if you like, you can set a border for your box. With tools on the Drawing toolbar, you can add shadow or 3-D styling.

Please don't try to use text boxes for the bulk of your text. That's not Word's native mode, so it's not going to work as well. Besides, it's not the best way to set up a book!

But if you want to stick text in an odd position, or have other text wrap around it, then a text box is the answer. For instance, with text boxes, you can place

"For normal text, don't use text boxes!"

headings or pithy quotes in the side margins for a classy look. Or create a *sidebar*—a box with supplementary information, like you often see in magazines. Or get automatic page numbers on the side by drawing a text box there while in Header and Footer View. Put your cursor in the box, then click the Insert Page Number toolbar button.

As with Word's graphics, one thing you can't do with a Word text box is fill a page and make your regular text flow from the page before to the page after. For that, you do need a page layout program.

Word's automatic text features—the creation of indexes, tables of contents, and such—ignore text in text boxes. But you can have most of the best of both worlds by placing text in *frames* instead. Though frames don't offer as many options, they can be moved around just like text boxes, while their text is still handled by automatic functions.

You can create a frame by first creating a text box, then double-clicking its border to call up the format dialog box. Go to the Text Box tab and click on "Convert to Frame." Or you can include frame properties as part of a style and simply apply the style to selected text. Double-clicking a frame border brings up a format dialog box.

Adding Borders and Backgrounds

You don't normally need a text box to place a border around text. Word lets you add one directly.

First create the text, select those paragraphs, then choose "Borders and Shading" from the Format menu. For inline paragraphs, this feature should provide all the options you need. To color the box, see the settings on the Shading tab.

You can also click on the Page Border tab of the dialog box to set up a border for every page in the document or only for those in one section. Unlike a text box, this border appears around the page as a visual element only, without constraining the text or interacting with it in any other way. Text will flow in and out as if the border wasn't there. (Shading is not available within page borders as it is within paragraph borders.)

A custom page border or background can easily be added to a page in the form of a drawing or a picture. In the graphic's format dialog box, choose the "Behind text" wrapping style and position the graphic on the page. Make sure that "Move object with text" is not selected. A drawing can be made semi-transparent, and on the Mac, a picture can too. To repeat the graphic throughout one or more sections, insert it while editing headers and footers.

Confusingly, Word's Background command was designed for Web documents, not for print, and on the Mac it will even switch you to Online Layout View. But later versions of Word also include a versatile Watermark feature for inserting a custom background throughout a document. In Windows, select "Printed Watermark" from the Background submenu on the Format menu. On the Mac, choose "Watermark" from the Insert menu. From the dialog box, you can import your picture and even select a "Washout" option to lighten it.

Adding Ornaments

O rnaments can add a nice touch to your book. For instance, Word has an automatic Drop Cap feature you might enjoy using for chapter beginnings in more stylish books.

Word's support for Unicode means that many fonts have characters you can use for pure design. You can also find such characters in the old symbol and dingbat fonts.

Ornaments can also be made from small imported graphics. Just place them inline or float them anywhere on the page. To make them repeat on succeeding pages, insert them in headers or footers.

Working with Word #5: Using Alignment Aids

Though Word lacks the variety of built-in alignment aids found in a page layout program, it does provide some assistance, and you can improvise more.

Word's basic alignment aid is a background grid, which you can set up and make visible from the Draw menu on the Drawing toolbar. The dialog box lets you set the grid interval and starting point, and also lets you choose whether objects will snap to the grid.

For more help with positioning, you can use Word's drawing function to create vertical and horizontal guide lines. On the Drawing toolbar, just choose the Line button, then drag your cursor either down or across your page, pressing the Shift key to keep your line from slanting. Afterward, you can move the line to wherever you need it, then delete it when you're through. Keep it arranged on top of text and other graphics by using commands from the Draw menu on the Drawing toolbar.

Other possible aids include rectangles you draw yourself and position behind text; page borders created with the Borders and Shading command on the Format menu; and text boxes formatted with visible lines around them. Just remember to remove your aids before sending the document to your print service!

9
Preparing for Print

All your work will be wasted if you don't get your book to your print service in usable form. Here's what you need to know.

Choosing a Print Service

Before committing to a print service, make sure it can handle what you plan to give it. If you want to submit your book as hard copy, make sure that's OK. If you want to submit it as PDF files, make sure the service handles them.

Print-on-demand services always take PDF files, and they're used to handling such files created from Word. The same should be true of any print service with a digital press. But it's always best to ask.

Centering Your Pages

In my chapter on document formatting, I advised you to set your document paper size to match your desired book page size. This is the best choice for checking your layout on screen, and it also lets you produce PDF files with pages at exact trim size. This format is now accepted and even preferred by most print services working with PDF.

Some print services, though, require you to center your book pages on a larger sheet—usually standard letter-size or A4. And some publishers prefer to set up their documents like that anyway, considering it easier than setting a custom paper size. Of course, this is your only practical option when preparing hard copy for scanning.

Centering your pages can seem tricky, but it's really not hard. First "Select All" to make sure your changes apply to the entire document. Then change your paper size to the dimensions of the larger sheet—usually back to your system's default. Again, this setting is in the Page Setup dialog box, on the Paper or Paper Size tab or pull-down menu.

Next, with the entire document still selected, enlarge your document margins to take up the slack on the enlarged page. Again, the Margins settings are in the dialog box for Page Setup (Windows) or Document Format (Mac). And you're done!

For instance, say you have to center your page on a letter-size sheet, $8\frac{1}{2} \times 11$ inches, and your book page is 6×9 inches with page margins of 1 inch top and bottom, and $\frac{3}{4}$ inch left and right. The larger sheet is $2\frac{1}{2}$ inches wider than the book page, or $1\frac{1}{4}$ inches on each side. So, you would add that $1\frac{1}{4}$ inches to your left and right document margins, making each of them a total of 2 inches.

Likewise with the height. The larger sheet is 2 inches taller than the book page, or 1 inch each on top and bottom. This inch is added to the top and bottom document margins, again for a total of 2 inches each. Don't forget to add the inch also to the header and footer margins.

If you've done everything right, you'll find that all your line and page endings are exactly the same as before. If not, go back and try again!

If you don't want to mess with all this, you can use Acrobat Professional to change this easily *after* your PDF file is made. I'll explain how later in this chapter.

Preparing Hard Copy

Though the standard in publishing today is to submit books to your print service as PDF files, it's still possible to send "hard copy"—printed pages that can be scanned. (Such pages used to be called *camera-ready copy* because they were photographed—but no longer.)

The key is to provide printouts of high quality. Among other things, that means no inkjet printing! You will have to use a laser printer to get smooth enough type. Use a good-quality white bond paper, such as designed for desktop printing or photocopying.

Hard copy is OK for type, line drawings, and sometimes even prescreened art. But if you have continuous-tone graphics like unscreened photos or paintings, your print service will have to process them separately. Contact your service to find out in what form to submit them.

You'll also need to leave room for them on the pages. To do this, just use Word to draw a rectangle of the exact size of the finished graphic, and place it in the exact position you want. To avoid confusion, you might want to type an identifying number for the graphic inside the box, or include a low-resolution clip of it with the words "For Position Only," or just "FPO."

This kind of graphics handling is available for traditional offset printing but not usually for print on demand. So if you're using POD for a book with such graphics, forget hard copy.

Preparing Word Files

Word was not designed for commercial publishing, and files in its own format are not suited to use by print services. But if you still prefer to send Word files directly and you find a service that accepts them, here are ways to minimize the danger.

• Try to prepare your file in the same Word version used by your print service. In particular, don't send a Windows file to be used on a Mac, or a Mac file to be used in Windows.

• If possible, embed your fonts directly in your file. In Word for Windows, this can be done for TrueType fonts with a setting in your Save Options. The feature is not currently available on the Mac.

• If you're not embedding your fonts, you will probably need to send them separately to your print service. These fonts are files in your computer's operating system, *not* in Word itself. For instance, in Windows, you access them through your Fonts control panel. For each typeface, be sure to include the files for all needed styles—plain, italic, and so on.

• If your fonts are embedded or you're sending them separately to your print service , make sure the "Use printer metrics" setting is turned *off* in your document's Compatibility Options or Preferences.

• If your fonts are *not* embedded and you're *not* sending them separately, make sure the "Use printer metrics" setting is turned *on*. Then ask your print service for its printer driver, install it in your system, and see that it's selected while you're formatting your document.

• Make sure your styles are not set for automatic update.

• If it does not make your document file unreasonably large, embed all graphics and other inserted objects.

Preparing PDF Files

PDF stands for "Portable Document Format," and its introduction has revolutionized the printing industry. Now, instead of supplying a print service with a myriad of connected text, illustration, and font files, or a pile of pasted-up sheets, a publisher can send just one file for the book interior and another for the cover. This has led not only to greater convenience but to greater reliability as well.

It has also led to being able to use Microsoft Word in publishing. Files in Word format are not suited for direct use on a commercial printing press, and most print services won't accept them. But properly convert those files to PDF, and Word can do just fine.

It all started with Adobe Acrobat, which is still the preeminent program for creating and working with PDF files. Acrobat now comes in two main editions, called Standard and Professional. Either one will produce the same high-quality PDF files. Those of you with a technical bent, though, will prefer Professional, as each new version has added a number of highly useful functions for analyzing, altering, and optimizing your files after creation. On the Mac, Professional is the *only* edition available.

Understandably, many new self publishers try to cut costs by using one of the numerous cheap or free PDF programs that now often substitute for Acrobat. The problem is that the files most of them produce are meant only for viewing and printing on the desktop, not for printing on a commercial press.

For straight text with no special characters or design elements, their files may work just fine. But the further your text departs from plain vanilla, the more chance that your Acrobat substitute may misinterpret or simply drop unusual elements. In the same way, the program may have trouble with high-resolution bitmap graphics and vector graphics, including charts, boxes, and shading. You may wind up losing more money on botched proofs than you would have spent on buying Acrobat in the first place—not to mention the frustration and waste of time.

It's certainly true, though, that Acrobat has become pricey. To save money, you could find an older version from an online software discounter, then either create your files with that version or use it to qualify for upgrade pricing on a newer one. Any Acrobat version back to 4 will create suitable files— that is, if it runs on your current operating system. And actually, to qualify for an upgrade, it doesn't have to run on your computer or even install, as long as you get the serial number.

You can also find older versions on eBay. But if the previous owner registered the program with Adobe, you may need to satisfy the company by submitting formal proof of the transfer of ownership before you upgrade. Also, when buying any software on eBay, you have to be on guard against pirated copies, which will not work for upgrading.

For limited use, you may find it practical to use Adobe's online PDF conversion service, either in a free trial or for a low monthly rate—but I haven't tried this myself. Find details at

createpdf.adobe.com

If you're considering a different PDF program, at least try to determine if other self publishers have used it reliably for this purpose. And if you go ahead with it, be sure to at least check the resulting files with the free Adobe Reader (formerly Acrobat Reader).

Personally, I consider Acrobat one of the basic and essential tools in a self publishing toolkit, and I wouldn't leave home without it. While the rest of this section includes general advice on PDF settings, the specific procedures I describe will be based on Acrobat.

Acrobat offers several ways to create a PDF file from a Word document. You can use PDFMaker, the plug-in that adds toolbar buttons to Word, as well as an extra menu in Word for Windows. You can use Word's Print command and select as your printer "Adobe PDF" or "Create Adobe PDF." Or use Word's Print command to save to a PostScript file, then process it with Acrobat's companion program, Acrobat Distiller.

With all these methods, it's Distiller that winds up doing the actual processing, and the output quality is the same. But in Word for Windows, PDFMaker is probably your best bet, especially if you're using a custom paper size. All necessary settings can be accessed from the Adobe PDF menu in Word and even saved as a preset option for future use. (The short PDFMaker toolbar, annoyingly placed on a row of its own, can be moved elsewhere to save space or else turned off, like any other toolbar, from the View menu.)

On the Mac, Acrobat's PDFMaker is less functional and well-behaved than it is in Windows. In fact, the best thing I can tell you might be how to get rid of it permanently. (Open your Microsoft Office folder, then "Office," then "Startup," then "Word." Remove the PDFMaker.dot file and replace it with an empty folder of the same name, preventing Acrobat from restoring the file.)

In Windows, if you choose to use the Print command and the Adobe PDF printer, you can change your settings by clicking on the Properties button in the Print dialog box. In fact, you'll need to do that each time if you're using a custom paper size, because you must set the printer's "Page Size" to match it. Conversion might go a bit faster if you select the option "Do not send fonts to 'Adobe PDF'" or "Rely on system fonts only, do not use document fonts," which limits where Acrobat looks for the fonts you tell it to embed—but leave this *off* if there's any chance the document includes embedded fonts not found on your computer. Back in the main Print dialog box, do *not* select "Print to file."

When using the Adobe PDF printer on the Mac, you can select various settings presets by choosing "PDF Options" from the pull-down menu. But you have to open Acrobat Distiller to add or edit your own.

If you're instead generating a PostScript file for Distiller, you can still choose the Adobe PDF printer. Other PostScript devices will work too, such as a generic Adobe print driver, or a driver supplied by your print service, or even your desktop laser printer. For Windows, though, your desktop printer probably won't allow settings to match custom paper sizes.

To generate the PostScript file in Windows, select "Print to file" in the Print dialog box. If you're using the Adobe PDF printer for this, make sure the printer properties option "Do not send fonts to 'Adobe PDF'" or "Rely on system fonts only" is *not* selected. To generate the file in Mac OS X 10.4, use the "Save PDF as PostScript" command on the Print dialog box's PDF menu. (Don't be confused by the command's name or placement—it has nothing to do with PDF.) In earlier versions of OS X, choose "Output Options" from the dialog box's main pull-down menu, then "Save as File" and "PostScript."

Note that Distiller for Mac OS X generates terribly bloated files, with separate font subsetting for each and every page. These files can take minutes to "Save As" when you work with them in the Acrobat program—in fact, you might think the application is hanging. Mac OS X's own PDF functions produce more streamlined files—but they may cause printing problems with some Unicode special characters or advanced graphics.

One PDF creation method no one should use is PDF-Writer, a simplified and inferior PDF converter that Adobe included with early versions of Acrobat before PDFMaker replaced it. The files created by PDFWriter are not suited to commercial printing.

Be sure to consult with your print service about the best settings to use for your PDF files, and then follow them unless you have good reason to do otherwise. Here are some general suggestions for producing files meant for commercial printing.

First, to speed things up and reduce file size, turn off any options for creating links, bookmarks, tags, or anything else not needed for print.

Choose to compress text and line art, if given the option. To compress other graphics, choose a lossless method like Zip or LZW. Make sure you don't "downsample" or antialias your images, unless you know that's what you want.

If you *must* compress your graphics with JPEG for smaller file size, choose maximum *quality* or minimum *compression*. These are two ways of saying the same thing—but be sure you know whether it's compression or quality that you're specifying. PDF settings dialogs don't always make this clear, and in older programs may even accidentally reverse them! To test this, try more than one setting, then use the one that produces the *largest* file.

To make sure your PDF files appear and print as you expect, choose to embed and subset *all* fonts, and remove all font names from Acrobat's "Never Embed" list. If asked for a percentage limit for subsetting, choose 100% (except with Acrobat 3, which should be told 99%). Subsetting prevents your print service's software from substituting a different version of the font.

If your Word document includes an EPS or PDF vector graphic with type, make sure the font has already been embedded in the graphic. Otherwise, the font might not make it into the PDF file.

It's important to use Acrobat (or the Adobe Reader) to check the fonts embedded in your PDF file. From the File menu, choose "Document Properties" and then "Fonts." If you don't see all expected fonts in the listing, try first scrolling through the document. What you want to read beside each font name is "Embedded Subset" or similar.

You may sometimes see *more* fonts listed than you expect—for instance, if you accidentally applied a font somewhere in the text, or copied text with a different font from another document. If so, you can find it in the text with Word's Find command. Put your cursor in the "Find what" box, but don't enter *anything,* not even a space! Instead, use the advanced Format settings at the bottom of that dialog box to choose the font you want to search for. To tell Word to replace that font with another, place your cursor in the "Replace with" box and use the advanced Format settings again.

Stray fonts can also be part of Word's default formatting of automatic elements, such as bullets or numbering in lists, or reference marks in footnotes or endnotes. Though Word lets you change this font in its dialog boxes for these automatic functions, there's generally no need if the font is embedding properly. You may remember, though, that I said fonts may *not* embed properly when used for automatic bullets and list numbers, which is one reason I advise adding such elements manually.

By the way, these fonts for automatic elements can't be found with the Find command, because they're not actually in the text! If you can't figure out where they are and *must* find them, first make a copy of the document just for testing. Then delete parts of the text, testing for the problem at each step, till you have it pinpointed.

Occasionally, you may find a font that is restricted so that it will not embed. In that case, you'll have to replace the font.

But this problem should not arise with fonts that came with your operating system, Word, or most other programs.

I mentioned before that Distiller for Mac OS X generates bloated files, and you'll see that in this fonts list, with a separate subset of each font for each page on which it appears. That makes a very long list! Also, Acrobat on the Mac may substitute Arial for Helvetica—but don't worry about that. The two typefaces are pretty much identical.

After you check your fonts in "Document Properties," other font problems may be revealed by a visual check of the document—that is, *if* you turn off Acrobat's option "Use local fonts" in the Page Display preferences. That way, Acrobat will display text solely with fonts that are either embedded in the file or that the program can generate itself, while ignoring fonts installed on your computer. In other words, you'll see the text as your print service will see it.

For black-and-white pages in print on demand, the best color setting for creating the PDF file is "Leave Color Unchanged." *Do not* convert from Word's native RGB to CMYK or grayscale when creating this file, because the type in your book will not translate to pure black. Today's digital presses can handle Word's RGB just fine when printing to black and white.

You *may* also be able to send this file for offset printing if you or your print service can clean it up. Acrobat Professional's print production tools are great for this. Use the "Convert Colors" command to change the file to grayscale or CMYK—but make sure you select the option "Preserve Black Objects" to keep the type pure black! (That option comes only with this command, and is not available when you first create the file.) Specify the color profile recommended by your print service.

After converting, you can check the results with Acrobat Professional's Output Preview. For this level of precision, make sure you first turn off all smoothing options in the program's

Page Display preferences. Otherwise, you'll see values that are in your display but not in your file.

What if you're creating pages in full color? As I said before, Word simply isn't suited to this kind of work, since it can't work natively in CMYK. Still, if you have Acrobat Professional to fix up the PDF file—and if close color accuracy is not a concern—you *might* get away with it. For such a case, again create your PDF file with color unchanged, then use "Convert Colors" to change it to CMYK, once again with "Preserve Black Objects" selected.

Acrobat Professional's Preflight feature can also be used to check for any other problems in the file, specifying the preflight profile that your print service recommends. Starting with version 8, Acrobat Professional can even automatically repair problems that it finds.

Acrobat lets you choose compatibility of your PDF file with various versions of the program. Choosing an earlier version helps ensure compatibility with your print service's software and may also turn off features that needlessly increase file size. The choice generally recommended for commercial printing is Acrobat 4—or as it is often specified, PDF 1.3, since that's the version Acrobat 4 uses to produce its files.

If your Word document produces multiple PDF files instead of one, it means you've applied differing paper size, orientation, or margin settings to different sections of your document. If that's not what you needed, first select your entire document, then go back to the Page Setup or Document Format dialog box and reenter the settings. Otherwise, you can merge the PDF files within Acrobat.

If you've created your document and PDF file for one paper size and need to convert it to another, you can change it with Acrobat Professional's Crop Pages command. (Don't confuse this with the Crop Tool.) Use the dialog box's "Change

Page Size" settings to center your pages on a larger sheet, or use the "Crop Margins" settings to trim off excess.

Acrobat Professional also lets you do some basic content editing—but in most cases, you're better off going back to your Word document and generating a new PDF file.

Placing Crop Marks

Though seldom needed for print on demand, your print service might otherwise ask you to add *crop marks* to your file or hard copy. These are short lines drawn outside the book page area at the corners to define where the sheet should be trimmed.

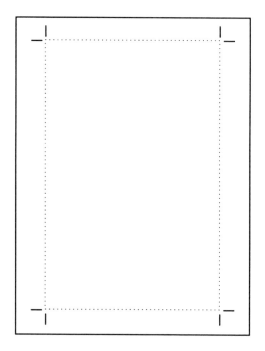

Crop marks

You might be asked to place these marks on the first page only, or throughout. One way is to add the crop marks to a PDF file itself. Acrobat Professional has this capability, starting in version 6.

Word itself has no feature for this, so if you don't have Acrobat Professional, you'll have to improvise. Probably the simplest way is to create a single graphic with marks for all four corners—a vector graphic, or at least a low-resolution bitmap, to keep down file size. This graphic can be floated on your first page, or chosen as a Watermark to appear throughout.

Since crop marks must appear outside the page area, the paper size of your file must be greater by at least enough to accommodate them. Of course, the added area should be equal on opposing sides so the book page stays centered on the sheet.

If you're submitting hard copy for scanning and don't want to add crop marks to your file, you can create a single page with all the marks and print out enough copies for all the pages of your book. Then put the sheets back in the printer and print your book over them. Or in a pinch, you can always draw the marks by hand!

Checking Your Work

Word's spelling and grammar checkers can be useful tools, but they can never completely replace careful proofing by eye. That's because their are weigh two many words that ken bee wrong even when spilled write. Not to @ mention >punctuation< errors %.

Checking your work on screen isn't good enough either. Errors are much harder to spot that way. For careful checking, print it out. Yes, printing out a book takes a lot of paper—but think of all the printed books that could be spoiled if you don't!

However much earlier checking you've done, be sure to carefully check your book in the final form destined for your printer. If you're sending PDF files, print those out. Make sure that italic and bold type has been preserved, and that your headers and footers have the correct text and position. Try to distance yourself from the text's meaning and instead see its "shape."

Finally, never pass up a chance to review a proof from your print service. Its printing press may have problems with your files that your desktop printer didn't. Find out before the book goes to press! And have a loupe or other magnifier on hand to examine type and graphics. Sometimes that's the only way to figure out why something looks wrong.

10
Creating a Cover

Book covers are best created in professional page layout programs, which handle color in the way needed for commercial printing. But in a pinch, you can certainly use Word to create simple covers for print on demand and limited or online sales. Here's how.

Setting Your Cover Size

A tricky part of creating a book cover in Word is that you must handle paper sizes larger than normal. The first step is to figure your exact cover dimensions.

For a paperback, of course, both the front and back cover sizes are the same as the book page size, or *trim size*—the size of the book after the edges are trimmed. Also to be included in the width is the *spine*—the narrow strip that faces out on bookshelves, printed between the front and back covers. The spine width is determined by the number of pages in your book and the pages per inch for the specific kind of paper your book will be printed on.

Your print service will have to tell you the pages per inch (ppi) for the paper you'll use. A typical number might be between 400 and 500. Keep in mind that you're counting *pages,* not sheets of paper. Each sheet used in the printed book counts as two pages, front and back.

To extend our example from my chapter on formatting your document, let's say we have a book with a trim size of 6 × 9 inches and a page count of 200, to be printed on paper with a thickness of 400 pages per inch. The cover width would be the sum of the widths of the front and back covers plus the spine—6 + ¼ + 6 inches, for a total of 12¼.

Our final cover size, then, would be 12¼ × 9 inches. (Remember, I'm giving width before height.) But almost always, the *paper* size has to be at least a bit bigger to allow for *bleed.* That's the area you place around the cover to allow the printing press to print beyond the cover edge.

Why would you need that? Well, printing presses aren't perfect. If you try to print a graphic right up *to* the edge, you stand a good chance of leaving a sliver of paper unprinted. So you need to hang the graphic a little *past* the edge and let the excess be trimmed off.

The same goes for a color background. Commercial book covers are always on white paper, with background color printed onto it. So you extend the color past the edge for safety.

An eighth-inch bleed at each edge is often recommended, but I generally use ¼ inch—to give me more leeway in spine measurement and also just to simplify the arithmetic. In any case, add the same bleed all around to make sure your cover is properly centered when printed. Of course, if you're *not* printing to the edge, you don't need bleed at all.

For our cover document, then, the paper size has to equal at least the cover size plus the bleed. In our example, with a ¼ inch bleed, the paper size would be 12¾ × 9½ inches. From top to bottom on the height, that's ¼ + 9 + ¼ inches. From left to right on the width, that's ¼ + 6 + ¼ + 6 + ¼ inches.

Set that size the same way you'd set any other custom paper size, as described in my chapter on formatting your document. Make sure you select landscape mode.

When working with inches in Windows, you may find you can create a cover PDF file only in quarter-inch increments. If your spine width throws this off, increase the paper width to the next appropriate dimension.

Setting Your Cover Margins

There's a simple trick that will make it easier to lay out your cover, and it's worth more than the price of this book in the trouble it will save you: Set up your cover as two columns.

Start by using Page Setup (Windows) or Document Format (Mac) to set your document margins. The left and right margins should match the width of your bleed area. For the book cover we're using as our example, that would mean a quarter-inch margin, left and right. For no bleed, those margins would be zero. If you increased the paper width to the next quarter-inch increment, add half the increase to each margin.

For each of the top and bottom margins, we want the bleed plus half an inch—¾ inch total, in our example. The half inch is the distance you're advised to keep important elements from the book edges—at least for print on demand.

Gutter, header, and footer margins should all be zero.

Next select the Columns command from the Format menu and choose "Two." Also select the option "Equal column width." (Do *not* select "Line between.") Then set the first column width to equal the trim width of your book cover. Set the spacing *between* columns to equal the width of your spine. In our example, those measurements are 6 inches and ¼ inch.

Back in the document, press the Return or Enter key, then add a Column Break at the cursor. Select All, then use the Paragraph Format dialog box to create indents of ½ inch at left and right. This again is the distance you want to keep things from the book edges.

You now have your back cover as your left column, and your front cover as your right column. You can easily add whatever text and graphics you like and automatically align them. And your spine goes between the columns!

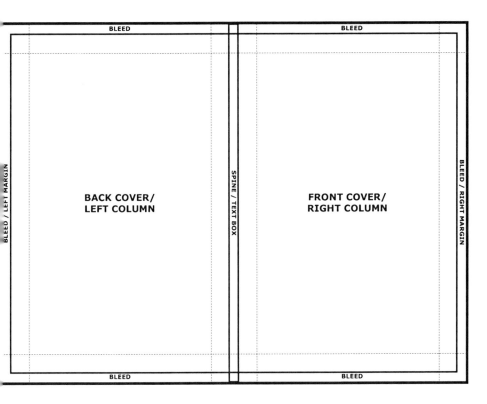

Cover Layout

Handling Cover Type

I've already discussed the problem of using Word's black type on full-color pages, and the same problem applies when printing a color cover by offset. But ironically, this is not usually a problem with print on demand—in fact, it becomes an asset.

In print on demand, black type for color covers is generally rasterized and screened, and most often antialiased too. In this situation, the "pure black" that gives the smoothest type in offset printing will actually produce rougher, fuzzier type than the "rich black" you normally get from Word.

Still, whether you're printing your cover on demand or else trying to print it by offset with a PDF file straight from Word, certain guidelines will help compensate for type quality somewhat below standard.

To start, you can avoid text in smaller sizes, since that's what looks the worst. For a book meant for limited sales or for selling online, the only cover text you really need is the title and your name.

A delicate typeface can be a problem even at larger sizes. You might want to restrict the cover type to a sans serif face, or at least a robust serif face, such as one designed for the Web. For most of my own covers, I've used Verdana. Also, placing type on a color background can help obscure roughness.

Because titles on covers are so large and prominent, their typographic weaknesses can be much more noticeable. So, you might want to spend extra time on them, looking at each letter pair to see if it needs kerning, and at each pair of lines to check linespacing. At times you might have to change something that's right if it just *looks* wrong.

To place text on the cover spine, create and format a text box, as described in my chapter on enhancing your layout. Of course, unless your spine is extremely wide, you'll want your text to run sideways. Set this up by selecting your text box and choosing "Text Direction" from the Format menu or clicking the "Change Text Direction" button on the Text Box toolbar. Be sure to choose the direction that's customary for your country—for instance, top to bottom for the U.S. and Canada, and bottom to top for the U.K.

Sticking with capital letters on the spine generally lets you use a larger font size for sideways text, because you don't have to worry about letters that hang down. And capital letters, as well as bolding, help make up for small text on narrow spines.

Handling Cover Graphics

Preparing individual graphics for a cover isn't much different than for interior pages, other than that the graphics are much more likely to be in color. But the glossy coating applied to covers makes colors a bit darker, so you might want to compensate by lightening your graphic a little—maybe 10% for the midtone levels on the histogram, *without* changing your black and white points.

All color graphics you insert in Word for your cover should originally be in RGB color mode. Ignore all advice to make them CMYK! Word would simply convert them to RGB anyway, which would waste your effort and give you a slight color shift into the bargain. At some point before printing, the image *will* be converted to CMYK, but don't worry about it yet.

Still, you do need to expect the change at some point, and when it happens, that too is bound to produce some color shift. So, you might want to avoid graphics in which color accuracy is critical—for instance, photos of people, since flesh tones are hard to get right. You'd probably want to avoid such finicky graphics anyway, since matching the print color with what you see on your monitor is always a challenge.

Don't forget that you can move graphics forward and back with the Arrange or Order command on the Draw menu of the Drawing toolbar.

Adding a Bar Code

If your book is to be handled by wholesalers, bookstores, or even the big online booksellers, your cover will need a bar code with the book's identifying ISBN (International Standard Book Number).

Most POD services will supply the bar code, with either your ISBN or theirs—and you should let them! Word's problem with black type in color documents applies to bar codes as well, but with these it's more critical. Bar codes are read by machines, and fuzzy edges can confuse them.

And Word isn't the only likely problem. For instance, a print-on-demand service will probably rasterize, antialias, and screen the cover you submit to make printing more efficient. This is almost guaranteed to degrade any bar code you send.

All in all, your best bet is to avoid the whole mess and let your service handle it. (A POD service, for instance, may add the bar code in vector type *after* it rasterizes your cover.) If you want the bar code in a certain spot, you can show that by placing a white box, with or without a border. Check with your service for minimum dimensions and distance from the edge.

If you need or decide to add your own, you'll find you would have to produce a fair number of them to justify paying the typical cost of bar code software. Instead, you can buy individual bar codes from any of a large number of services, including R. R. Bowker, the U.S. company that supplies ISBNs.

www.bowker.com

Or try the free online bar code generator used by many self publishers, at

www.tux.org/~milgram/bookland

Preparing Your Cover for Print

As with your book pages, your print service may ask you to submit your cover positioned on a larger sheet in a standard size—probably *tabloid,* 11 × 17 inches. Again as with your book pages, you can do this by adding to the document margins on all sides. (Word will handle any paper size up to 22 inches in either direction.) Or you can use the Crop Pages command in Acrobat Professional.

Though I recommend creating your cover as a PDF file, you could instead produce it as hard copy for scanning. Unless you own a humungous desktop printer, the best way would be to create the front and back covers and spine as three separate pieces. It shouldn't be hard then to get your print service or someone else to scan the pieces and combine them.

For offset printing, hard copy covers must have their continuous-tone graphics submitted separately. Also, with some presses and cover designs, you can get cleaner color type by submitting it in black and white and specifying a "spot color."

For print on demand, the hard copy must be complete with all graphics and type in final color—and the understanding that you'll be losing some quality. If producing your copy on an inkjet, use glossy photo paper, and settings for highest quality.

Though I've already discussed creating a PDF file from a Word document, creating one from your cover can be tricky because of size and orientation, as well as color.

Your best bet is to use PDFMaker, the set of commands and toolbar buttons that Acrobat adds to Word itself. This will avoid any problem arising from size or orientation. On the Mac, first use Page Setup to format the file specifically for the Adobe PDF printer, and open Distiller to make sure it has the settings you'll need for your cover.

If you're not using PDFMaker, there's one frustrating problem you might have when producing a PDF cover file. Sometimes Acrobat decides it knows more about your document than you do and insists on rotating it into portrait mode. This is the downside of an otherwise helpful feature called Auto-Rotate. Acrobat looks for text near the beginning of the document to help it decide how to orient the page. If there's no text close enough to the beginning, Acrobat uses portrait mode, the default.

Sometimes covers do not include any text near enough to the beginning to tip off Acrobat. Or Acrobat might take its cue from your spine text, if that's what it reads first. If you have this problem, try adding a little text at the top left or elsewhere on your back cover. You could hide the text behind a graphic, or make it invisible by setting its color to exactly match the background. Or just add "BAR CODE HERE" to a box you've inserted on the back cover to show positioning.

If you're adding crop marks, be sure to set them so they show that the bleed area should be trimmed off.

You'll need to convert the color of your cover from Word's RGB to the CMYK used by commercial presses. The simplest way to do this is to tell Acrobat to convert all color to CMYK when it creates the PDF file.

This will give you a "rich black"—more black than anything else but with other colors added. The alternative is "pure black," with complete black coverage and no other colors mixed in. You can get this the way I prescribed for color interiors: Leave the color unchanged when you create your PDF file, then use Acrobat's "Convert Colors" command with the option "Preserve Black Objects."

In offset printing, rich black is generally preferred for larger cover type, since—as the name implies—it looks more full-bodied. But with the margin of error that comes from multiple inks being applied, it does make the type edges less distinct, which becomes a problem as the type gets smaller and more delicate. So, for smaller type, pure black is preferred.

With digital printing, such as for print on demand, the situation is different. In most cases, a POD service converts your cover to a single bitmap graphic with antialiasing, then screens the whole thing. Pure black type then comes out a bit fuzzy and blurred, while rich black type has a smoother edge. So, for print on demand, the simpler way of converting to CMYK will be better. Acrobat's default formulation for rich black—90% black coverage, 300% total—may not be exactly what your print service wants, but it should be close enough.

Technically, when preparing your file for one of today's digital presses, you shouldn't have to convert the color at all— the press itself can convert from RGB to CMYK when it prints. But if you do it yourself ahead of time, you'll at least be able to check the results and make sure they're acceptable. In fact, your print service may insist on a CMYK file for this very reason—they don't want the blame if you're disappointed!

If you're using print on demand and want more control over how your cover will print, you can convert your PDF file to a bitmap graphic yourself by importing it into Photoshop (not Photoshop Elements), making sure that CMYK color mode is selected. Also on import, you can choose antialiasing to give slightly smoother but less distinct type, or no antialiasing for type that's slightly sharper but rougher. (You may not see much or any difference, though, with the naked eye.)

Once your cover is in Photoshop, you can change its rich black to any formulation you like. Just use the Paint Bucket tool with minimal tolerance and the "Contiguous" option turned *off*. Be careful *not* to apply Photoshop's "registration black," which gives 100% coverage of each color. When you're finished, save the file as PDF and send off.

Checking Your Cover

Covers should be checked inch by inch and lived with for several days before you send them out. It's amazing how many ways you can find to improve a cover if you stare at it often enough. And on a cover, there's no room for any error.

To help you see the design and to check measurements, you might want to create a test PDF document with a border around the trim area. This can be created in Word as a Page Border, setting it to appear at a distance from the edge that's equal to the width of the bleed. Just remember to remove the border before creating your final PDF file!

Author Online!

For updates and more resources,
visit Aaron Shepard's Publishing Page at

www.aaronshep.com/publishing

For Further Help

Though Aaron is glad to receive feedback from readers, he cannot provide private technical assistance with Word. For further help, please see the resources listed at the end of this book or on his Web site.

Resources

Here are a few more resources to help you with book design and production, and with Microsoft Word.

Books

The Complete Manual of Typography: A Guide to Setting Perfect Type, by James Felici, Adobe, 2003. A top-flight reference. Felici understands not only traditional typography but also how it has translated to the computer.

The Complete Idiot's Guide to Self-Publishing, by Jennifer Basye Sander, Alpha, 2005. Includes an excellent discussion of what goes into creating and producing a commercial book.

The Chicago Manual of Style, University of Chicago, various years. The book publishing industry's standard reference for everything from grammar to the parts of a book.

The Official Adobe Print Publishing Guide, Second Edition, by Brian P. Lawler, Adobe, 2005. A good book for learning about basic book production technology and terminology, especially in regards to graphics. It will help you understand what your printer needs and wants from you.

Print on Demand: A Graphics Handbook, by Lon Barfield and Peter Maxwell, Bosko Books, 2005. Shows samples of graphics and type as printed by Lightning Source, the dominant U.S. POD print service.

Better Gray in Print on Demand, by Martin Koch, Verlag Martin Koch, 2006. Tips on how to draw out the max from your photos. The samples are stunning. The more advanced tips require a professional program like Photoshop (not Photoshop Elements), and some skill in using it. This book is being frequently revised and may also soon be renamed.

Word Bible, series, by Brent Heslop, et. al., Wiley. If you're producing books with Word, you'll want the most complete program documentation you can find. This title, with new editions for each major Word version for Windows, is excellent. In fact, Mac Word users might want it too, for its comprehensive documentation of features common to both versions.

Using Microsoft Word, Special Edition, series, by Bill Camarda, et. al., Que. Another excellent series of comprehensive manuals for specific versions of Word for Windows.

Office for Macintosh: The Missing Manual, series, O'Reilly. Sadly, there's nothing for Mac Word that equals the Word Bible series or the Using Microsoft Word series, but this is a step in that direction.

Take Control of What's New in Word, series, by Matt Neuburg, TidBITS. For Mac Word. Neuburg is great at plumbing the depths of new features. Available primarily as ebooks. Best ordering is from the publisher at www.takecontrolbooks.com.

Web Sites

Aaron Shepard's Publishing Page. My own collection of resources for self publishing, desktop publishing, and print on demand, including updates for this book. Also, sign up for my email bulletin to receive notice of further online updates and new editions.

www.aaronshep.com/publishing

Microsoft Word MVP FAQ Site. An independent site that features extensive advice. It's developed and maintained by the community of Microsoft "Most Valuable Professionals," which includes many prominent Word consultants. Among its many resources is Clive Huggan's monumental and frequently-updated ebook for Mac Word, *Bend Word to Your Will.*

word.mvps.org

Microsoft Office Online. Microsoft's collection of online resources for Word for Windows and other Office programs.

office.microsoft.com

Mactopia. Microsoft's site for the Mac versions of Word and other programs.

www.microsoft.com/mac

Planet PDF. Many resources for those creating or manipulating PDF files.

www.planetpdf.com

Newsgroups

microsoft.public.word.docmanagement
microsoft.public.word.pagelayout
microsoft.public.mac.office.word

These are the newsgroups most useful to publishers among a number of official ones hosted by Microsoft to provide help with Word. For a fuller and updated listing—plus handy links to Web-based interfaces for those without a newsreading program—look on the Word MVP or Microsoft Office Online sites listed earlier.

Email Discussion Lists

Word_DocDesign. For help with preparing books and other complex documents in Word.

groups.yahoo.com/group/Word_DocDesign

WORD-MS. For general help with Word.

groups.yahoo.com/group/word-ms

WORD-PC. For help with Word for Windows.

subscribe word-pc *firstname lastname*
listserv@listserv.liv.ac.uk

Newsletters

WordTips. A helpful email newsletter about Word for Windows.

wordtips.vitalnews.com

Woody's Office Watch. For Office for Windows.

www.office-watch.com/office

Editorium Update. Topical discussions on using Word for typesetting and other purposes. Mostly for Windows, but includes some Mac info. May not be issued regularly at present.

www.editorium.com/newsletr.htm

Index

Aaron Shepard's Publishing
Page, 11, 12, 144, 148
Adobe Acrobat, 10, 32, 50, 57,
97, 116, 119, 120, 121, 122,
123, 124, 125, 126, 127, 128,
129, 140, 141, 142
Adobe Acrobat Distiller, 121,
122, 125, 140
Adobe Illustrator, 96
Adobe InDesign, 9, 36, 63, 75
Adobe PageMaker, 9, 75
Adobe Photoshop and
Photoshop Elements, 96, 142,
146
Adobe Reader, 120, 124
antialiasing, 101, 123, 136, 139,
142
ASCII (text encoding), 48
AutoComplete, 20
AutoCorrect, 20, 44, 46, 48
AutoCorrect Options buttons,
20
AutoFormat, 20, 44, 45, 48, 49,
52
AutoRecover, 15
AutoText, 20
background saves, 15
backgrounds, 109, 129
backups, 12, 23, 42
bar codes, 139
binding and bindings, 32, 34
bitmap graphics, 12, 26, 96, 97,
98, 100, 101, 109, 110, 120

black and white (color mode),
12, 96, 97, 100, 101, 125, 138,
140
Blank Document template, 41
bleed and bleeding, 132, 133,
134, 141, 143
block quotes, 53, 54
bold font style, 51, 57, 66, 130
book covers, 58, 72, 97, 119, 131,
132, 133, 134, 136, 137, 138,
139, 140, 141, 142, 143
*Books, Typography, and
Microsoft Word*, 11
borders, 107, 108, 109, 112, 139,
143
Borders and Shading dialog box,
109, 112
bullets, 21, 80, 124
camera-ready copy, 117
cameras, digital, 96, 97
caption numbering, 85
chapters, 27, 35, 36, 37, 84
Character Palette (Mac), 48
Character Spacing, 61, 72, 76
Chicago Manual of Style, The,
35, 146
CID Type 2 (character
encoding), 50
CMYK (color mode), 97, 101,
125, 126, 138, 141, 142
colons, 52
color modes, 96, 97, 138, 141,
142

column breaks, 40
columns, 40, 57, 64, 67, 75, 88, 90, 93, 134
comb binding, 34
commas, 51
Compatibility Options or Preferences, 16, 17, 22, 54, 63, 73, 118
Complete Idiot's Guide to Self-Publishing, The, 35, 146
Complete Manual of Typography, The, 10, 146
compression, 97, 98, 123
concordance, 88, 89, 91, 92, 93
copyright page, 35
corruption, file or document, 12, 15, 21, 22, 30, 38, 42, 80
crop marks, 128, 129, 141
cross-references, 10, 85
Custom Paper Size panel (Mac), 32
Customize dialog box, 18
dashes, 45
descreening, 98
Document Format dialog box (Mac), 10, 33, 37, 39, 78, 115, 119, 126, 134
Document Map, 27
double primes, 49
draft output (Windows), 16
draw programs, 96
drawing canvas, 15, 96, 107
drawing objects, 96, 120, 123, 129
Drawing toolbar, 103, 107, 112, 138
drop caps, 111
ellipses, 46
em dashes, 45
em spaces, 52, 90
en dashes, 45
en spaces, 52

endnotes, 10, 84, 124
EPS (graphics file format), 101, 123
Fast Saves, 15, 22
Felici, James, 10, 146
fields and field codes, 44, 76, 85, 93
file locations, 22, 23, 42
files, Microsoft Word, 15, 17, 100, 118
Font Book (Mac), 58
Font Format dialog box, 61, 72, 76
font size, 58, 59, 60, 64, 66, 74, 93, 137
fonts and typefaces, 9, 15, 26, 33, 46, 48, 49, 50, 51, 52, 56, 57, 58, 59, 60, 61, 62, 64, 66, 68, 74, 80, 93, 111, 118, 119, 121, 122, 123, 124, 125, 132, 136, 137
Fonts control panel (Windows), 58, 118
footers, 26, 27, 34, 35, 36, 37, 39, 81, 82, 83, 103, 107, 109, 111, 116, 130, 134
footnotes, 10, 82, 84, 124
formatting, revealing, 28, 92, 102
formatting, tracking, 15, 22
fraction slashes or bars, 49, 50
fractional widths (Mac), 16
fractions, 20, 49, 50, 90
frames, 107, 108
French (language), 49, 56
General Options or Preferences, 96
Georgia (typeface), 50, 58, 59, 62, 68
German (language), 49
GIF (graphics file and compression format), 97

grammar, checking, 16, 73, 130, 146

graphics and graphics editing, 9, 12, 15, 25, 26, 30, 34, 60, 77, 95, 96, 97, 98, 99, 100, 101, 102, 103, 106, 107, 108, 109, 110, 111, 112, 117, 118, 119, 122, 123, 129, 130, 132, 134, 138, 140, 141, 142, 146

grayscale (color mode), 96, 97, 98, 100, 101, 125

grid, alignment, 112

gutter, 33, 34, 134

hard copy, 114, 115, 117, 128, 129, 140

Header and Footer toolbar, 81

headers, 26, 27, 34, 35, 36, 37, 39, 81, 82, 83, 103, 107, 109, 111, 116, 130, 134

headings, 27, 34, 39, 51, 54, 56, 57, 60, 61, 64, 65, 67, 79, 85, 89, 107

headings, run-in, 51

histogram, 98, 138

HTML paragraph auto spacing, 17, 54

hyphenation, 64, 66, 73, 74, 75

hyphens, 45, 64, 73, 74

inch marks, 49

indents and indenting, 33, 34, 53, 67, 68, 75, 93, 134

Index and Tables dialog box, 92, 93

Index tab, 92

indexes and indexing, 10, 53, 85, 87, 88, 89, 90, 91, 92, 93, 108, 153

international characters, 49

International Standard Book Number (ISBN), 139

italic font style, 49, 51, 89, 90

JPEG (graphics file and compression format), 97, 98, 123

justification and justifying, 17, 46, 61, 63, 64, 75, 76, 77, 80, 139

justification like WordPerfect, 17, 63

justification, vertical, 77, 78

kerning, 50, 61, 62, 72, 136

keyboard shortcuts, 18, 48, 49, 51

Language dialog box, 73

languages, foreign, 49, 74

Layout tab, 34, 36, 39, 77

letterspacing, 61, 72, 76

levels controls (in photo-paint programs), 98

Line and Page Breaks tab, 64, 65, 77

line art, 97, 98, 123

line endings, 73, 76, 77

linespacing, 60, 66, 77, 78, 101, 136

list numbering and bulleting, 21, 80, 124

Live Word Count, 16

LZW (graphics compression format), 98, 123

Mac OS 9, 11, 12

Mac OS X, 48, 50, 58, 122, 125

macros, 15

Manual Line Break, 73, 75, 76

Manual Page Break, 77, 78, 92

margins, 31, 33, 34, 52, 63, 73, 101, 107, 115, 116, 126, 127, 134, 140

Master Documents, 21, 30

math symbols, 50

memory, 25

menus and menu items, 15, 18, 19, 41, 107

Microsoft Word 2000
(Windows), 12
Microsoft Word 2001 (Mac), 11,
12
Microsoft Word 2003
(Windows), 12, 146
Microsoft Word 2004 (Mac), 11,
12, 16, 20, 63, 82, 91, 101
Microsoft Word 2007
(Windows), 11, 12
Microsoft Word 2008 (Mac), 11,
12
Microsoft Word 6 (Mac), 12
Microsoft Word 97 (Windows),
12
Microsoft Word 98 (Mac), 11, 12
Microsoft Word for the Mac, 11,
12, 15, 16, 18, 20, 23, 24, 26,
28, 32, 33, 36, 37, 39, 41, 45,
46, 48, 50, 51, 57, 58, 61, 63,
67, 73, 74, 78, 80, 82, 91, 93,
101, 109, 115, 118, 119, 121,
122, 125, 134, 140, 147, 148,
151
Microsoft Word for Windows,
11, 12, 15, 16, 17, 18, 22, 23,
24, 26, 28, 32, 33, 36, 37, 39,
45, 46, 48, 51, 52, 58, 63, 67,
73, 74, 78, 85, 91, 93, 96, 100,
101, 107, 109, 115, 118, 121,
122, 133, 134, 146, 147, 148,
150, 151
minus sign, 50
minute marks, 49
mirror margins, 34
monitors, computer, 96
monospace fonts and typefaces,
46, 56
Multiple Pages button, 27
multiplication sign, 50
Nonbreaking Hyphen, 73, 74

Nonbreaking Space, 46, 47, 52,
73, 74
Normal style, 68
Normal template (Normal.dot),
41, 42
Normal View, 16, 26, 28, 37, 40,
67, 81, 82, 84
No-Width Non Break, 74
No-Width Optional Break
(Windows), 74
numerals, 49
numerals, Roman, 83
Office Assistant, 18
*Official Adobe Print Publishing
Guide, The*, 99, 146
Online Layout View, 109
OpenType (font format), 57
Optional Hyphen, 28, 73, 75
options (Windows), 15, 16, 17,
18, 20, 22, 23, 42, 44, 49, 54,
63, 65, 68, 73, 78, 84, 85, 90,
93, 100, 101, 103, 107, 108,
109, 110, 115, 118, 121, 122,
123, 125, 134
Organizer, 42, 69
ornaments, 111
orphans, 65, 77
Outline View, 27
Page Border tab, 109, 143
page borders, 109, 112, 143
page breaks, 28, 35, 82, 92
page endings, 65, 77, 116
page layout programs, 9, 10, 29,
30, 32, 33, 36, 39, 40, 55, 57,
61, 71, 78, 84, 97, 101, 102,
103, 105, 107, 108, 112, 131
Page Layout View (Mac), 26, 81
Page Number Format dialog
box, 92
page numbers and numbering,
39, 83, 85, 86, 87, 92, 93, 107

Page Setup dialog box, 32, 33, 36, 37, 39, 77, 115, 126, 134, 140
page size, 31, 33, 59, 115, 132
pages per inch (ppi), 97, 101, 132
pages, odd and even, 27, 35, 39, 82, 83, 102
paper color, 98
Paper or Paper Size tab, 32, 115
paper size, 27, 31, 32, 115, 121, 122, 126, 129, 132, 133, 140
paperbacks, 59, 132
Paragraph Format dialog box, 33, 34, 53, 54, 60, 63, 64, 65, 77, 134
paragraphs and paragraphing, 16, 17, 22, 27, 28, 33, 34, 37, 51, 53, 54, 60, 63, 64, 65, 66, 67, 68, 69, 73, 75, 76, 77, 78, 80, 82, 101, 102, 109, 134
paragraphs, block, 53, 54
paragraphs, hanging, 53
paragraphs, indented, 53
paragraphs, keeping together, 77
paragraphs, keeping with next, 77
parentheses, 48
PDFMaker (Acrobat Word plug-in), 121, 123, 140, 141
PDFWriter (Acrobat accessory), 122
periods, 46, 51
photo-paint programs, 96, 98
photos, 96, 97, 98, 117, 138, 140, 146
pictures, 12, 26, 96, 97, 98, 100, 101, 109, 110, 120
placeholders, picture/image, 103
plus sign, 50

Portable Document Format (PDF), 10, 17, 31, 32, 50, 57, 58, 80, 85, 97, 100, 114, 115, 116, 117, 119, 120, 121, 122, 123, 124, 125, 126, 127, 128, 130, 133, 136, 140, 141, 142, 143, 148
PostScript (font format), 57
PostScript (printer language), 57, 121, 122
preferences (Mac), 15, 22, 23, 26, 28, 42, 48, 54, 63, 67, 73, 85, 90, 92, 102, 103, 118, 125, 126
preflighting, 126
primes, 49
Print Layout View (Windows), 26, 28, 40, 81, 84, 101, 102
print on demand (POD), 32, 33, 58, 98, 99, 114, 117, 128, 131, 133, 134, 136, 139, 140, 142, 146, 148
Print Options or Preferences, 85
Print Preview, 26, 27, 32, 40, 85, 101
printer drivers, 17, 118
printer metrics, 17, 118
printers, desktop, 10, 17, 50, 122, 130, 140
printing presses, 10, 28, 50, 58, 93, 97, 98, 107, 114, 119, 125, 130, 132, 134, 141, 142
printing services, 17, 32, 98
printing, black-and-white, 96
proofs and proofing, 50, 73, 120, 130
proportional fonts and typefaces, 46, 56
punctuation (general), 44, 46, 130
QuarkXPress, 9

quotation marks, 20, 44, 49, 90, 107

ranges, numerical, 45, 88, 98, 99

resolution, graphics, 26, 58, 97, 98, 101

Reveal Formatting task pane, 28

RGB (color mode), 96, 97, 125, 138, 141, 142

rulers, 33, 34, 52, 53

sans-serif fonts and typefaces, 56, 57, 136

Save Options or Preferences, 118

scanners and scanning, 96, 97, 98, 115, 117, 129, 140

screens and screening, 26, 31, 32, 57, 85, 96, 98, 102, 115, 130, 136, 139

sections and section breaks, 22, 28, 36, 37, 38, 39, 40, 81, 82, 84, 92, 109, 126

sentences, 16, 47, 52, 89, 92

serif fonts and typefaces, 56, 57, 136

shading, 85, 109, 120

Shading tab, 109

sharpening (for pictures), 98

Show/Hide button, 28, 92

sidebars, 107

slashes, 49, 74

smart cut and paste, 16

smart quotes, 20, 44, 49

spaces, 16, 28, 45, 46, 47, 52, 53, 60, 73, 74, 75, 80, 90, 124

Spacing Before and After, 17, 54, 60, 66

Special Characters tab, 48, 52, 73, 74

spelling and grammar, checking, 16, 73, 130, 146

spine, cover, 132, 133, 134, 137, 140, 141

Style Area, 67

Style Gallery, 42, 69

styles, 15, 21, 27, 35, 41, 42, 51, 54, 57, 61, 64, 65, 66, 67, 68, 69, 73, 77, 80, 85, 101, 108, 109, 118

Styles and Formatting panel (Windows), 67

Styles pane (Mac), 67

subheads, 51

subscripts, 49

superscripts, 49

Symbol dialog box, 44, 45, 46, 48, 50, 52, 73, 74, 80

tables, 10, 34, 35, 40, 52, 67, 85, 88, 90, 91, 92, 106, 108

tables of contents, 10, 35, 85, 91, 92, 108

Take Control of What's New in Word 2004, 48

templates, 17, 22, 23, 41, 42, 68, 69

text boxes, 26, 33, 40, 107, 108, 109, 112, 137

TIFF (graphics file format), 98

Times New Roman and Times (typefaces), 57, 59, 68

title page, 35, 61, 72, 78, 81, 83, 91

titles, 34, 35, 39, 57, 61, 66, 72, 78, 81, 83, 91, 136, 147

titles, book, 39, 90

titles, chapter, 51, 66

toolbars and toolbar buttons, 18, 19, 41, 121, 140

Track Changes, 21

tracking (letterspacing), 61

trim size, 31, 32, 99, 115, 132

TrueType (font format), 57, 118

Type 3, PostScript (font format), 57

underlining, 51

Unicode (text encoding), 48, 49, 50, 58, 74, 111, 122
Unicode Hex Input keyboard layout (Mac), 48
uninterrupted power supply (UPS), 24
unsharp mask, 98
updates and updating, 14, 42, 88
vector graphics, 96, 120, 123, 129
Verdana (typeface), 58, 62, 68, 136
Versions, 21
Vertical Alignment, 77
View Options or Preferences, 26, 28, 67, 82, 85, 92, 102, 103
views, 16, 18, 22, 23, 26, 27, 28, 67, 81, 82, 84, 85, 92, 102, 103, 107, 121

virgules, 49
viruses, 15, 24
Watermark, 109, 129
widows, 65, 77
windows, adding and splitting, 27
word count, 16
Word Help, 11, 14, 18, 28, 42, 48, 49, 144
word processors, 9, 43, 55, 61, 71, 75
wordspacing, 61, 72, 76
WYSIWYG font and style menus (Mac), 15
XML, 22
Zero Width Space, 74
Zip (graphics compression format), 98, 123

About the Author

Aaron Shepard has been making his living from self publishing for years and loving it (mostly). On the side, he is an award-winning children's author with numerous picture books from major publishers. Aaron lives in Olympia, Washington, with his wife and fellow author, Anne L. Watson.

Version History

1.0   January 6, 2006
1.1   January 15, 2006
1.2   February 17, 2006
1.3   February 24, 2006
1.4   March 9, 2006
1.5   June 6, 2006
1.6   April 6, 2007
1.7   April 10, 2007
1.8   June 8, 2007
1.9   October 12, 2007
1.10   November 30, 2007
1.11   December 26, 2007

Printed in the United States
99543LV00004B/12/A

9 780938 497332